FREE bonus material downloadable to your computer.
Visit: **www.hybridpublications.com**
Registration is free and easy.
Your registration code is RP659.

How To Crack Music Theory

WISE PUBLICATIONS

part of The Music Sales Group

London / New York / Paris / Sydney / Copenhagen / Berlin / Madrid / Tokyo

Published by
Wise Publications
14-15 Berners Street, London W1T 3LJ, UK.

Exclusive Distributors:
Music Sales Limited
Distribution Centre, Newmarket Road,
Bury St Edmunds, Suffolk IP33 3YB, UK.
Music Sales Corporation
257 Park Avenue South, New York, NY 10010,
United States of America.
Music Sales Pty Limited
20 Resolution Drive, Caringbah, NSW 2229, Australia.

Order No. AM991716
ISBN 978-1-84772-262-1
This book © Copyright 2009 Wise Publications,
a division of Music Sales Limited.

Text by James Sleigh.
Music examples by Mike Sheppard.
Audio examples arranged and recorded by Mike Sheppard.
Book layout and design by Artemis Music Limited.
(www.artemismusic.com)
Edited by Rachel Payne.
Cover design by Michael Bell Design.
Cover blocks framework image courtesy of Konstantinos Kokkinis/Fotolia.
Printed in the EU.

Contents

Introduction   9

Chapter 1:   The Minor Scale   **11**
  Accidentals   11
  Intervals   12
  The major scale   13
  From major to minor   16
  Harmonising the natural minor scale   18
  The perfect cadence in major keys   19
  The perfect cadence in minor keys   20
  The harmonic minor scale   21
  The melodic minor scale   23

Chapter 2:   Key Signatures   **25**
  Flat key signatures   26
  The circle of fifths   27
  Some good news   28
  Enharmonic equivalents   30
  Double sharps and double flats   34
  Cancelling double sharps and flats   35
  Major and minor key signatures   36

Chapter 3:   Rhythm   **39**
  The full set of note values   41
  The breve   42
  Triplets   44
  Duplets   45
  Rhythm notation – summary   48

Chapter 4:   Clefs   **51**
  The alto clef   53
  The tenor clef   55
  Tips and tricks   57
  The family of clefs   58
  Short score and open score   60

Chapter 5:   Transposing   **63**
  Non-octave transpositions   66
  Transposing instruments   70
  Transposition exercises   73
  Lesser-known transposing instruments   75

Contents

Chapter 6:   Time Signatures   77
Grouping notes in compound time   79
Rests in compound time   81
Counting in minims   83
Counting in semiquavers   85
Irregular time signatures   86
Beams and ties in irregular time signatures   88

Chapter 7:   General Musicianship   91
The instruments of the orchestra   91
Organisation of the orchestra   92
The string family   93
String techniques   94
The woodwind family   97
The brass family   100
The percussion family   103
Instruments from outside the classical tradition   104
Guitar notation   106

Chapter 8:   Composition (Part 1)   111
Questions and answers   111
Learn from the masters   114

Chapter 9:   Performance   117
Tempo and mood   118
Grace notes and trills   120
Mordents and turns   121
Writing out ornaments   124
Exercises   127

Chapter 10:   Harmony   129
Harmonising the minor scale   130
Adding the seventh   131
Exercises   134
Cadences   136
Cadences, keys and modulation   138
Suspensions   141
Double suspensions   143
Further exploration   144

Chapter 11:   Composition (Part 2)   147
Writing answering melodies   148
Writing a melody to given words   151
Exercises and ideas   154

Worksheet answers   159

Index   169

Audio examples

Chapter 1: The Minor Scale

Audio track 1	16
Audio track 2	18
Audio track 3	19
Audio track 4	20
Audio track 5	20
Audio track 6	21
Audio track 7	23

Chapter 3: Rhythm

Audio track 8	45
Audio track 9	46

Chapter 5: Transposing

Audio track 10	63
Audio track 11	66
Audio track 12	67
Audio track 13	67
Audio track 14	68

Chapter 6: Time Signatures

Audio track 15	77
Audio track 16	78
Audio track 17	78
Audio track 18	83
Audio track 19	87

Chapter 8: Composition
(Part 1)

Audio track 20	111
Audio track 21	112
Audio track 22	112
Audio track 23	113
Audio track 24	113

Chapter 9: Performance

Audio track 25	120
Audio track 26	123

Chapter 10: Harmony

Audio track 27	129
Audio track 28	131
Audio track 29	132
Audio track 30	132
Audio track 31	137
Audio track 32	137
Audio track 33	142
Audio track 34	143

Chapter 11: Composition
(Part 2)

Audio track 35	150
Audio track 36	154

Audio examples

All the audio examples referred to in this book can be found at **www.hybrid publications.com**

Look out for the audio track logo (see below). Every time you see it, check out the website for audio clips that will demonstrate the music examples.

Audio track

Introduction

Our aim in writing this book

This book is is a follow-up to our first book on music theory, called simply 'How To Read Music'. When writing it, we started with the aim of cutting through the mystery and confusion surrounding music notation to make it as easy as possible to understand how it works. Our approach was essentially a practical one – we believe that music notation is a tool that musicians use to help them to achieve their musical aims. As such, it shouldn't be viewed as a chore that has to be endured or done under duress – in the long run it's going to make your life as a musician easier, so it's in your interest to invest a little time and effort in learning about it.

In this book we want to continue from where we finished 'How To Read Music' and explore further into the world of music theory. Each chapter will begin with a brief recap of the material covered in the first book before introducing new concepts and areas. We'll also discuss wider areas of musical knowledge that might be described as making up 'general musicianship'. The two books together contain all the information you would need to get to roughly Grade 5 standard in the Associated Board's Music Theory Exams.

Just as in 'How To Read Music' we will use recordings to allow you to hear what individual bits of notation and music theory actually sound like. Every time you see an Audio track icon in the sidebar, that means that there is an accompanying audio example that demonstrates something in the text. We hope that this will allow you to make the connection between real music and what can sometimes seem to be quite abstract bits of music theory. All the audio examples can be found online here: **www.hybridpublications.com**. You'll also find all sorts of other supplementary material that will help you to get the most out of this book. For example, answers to the various exercises in the book are available there to download, along with lots of other extra material. Whenever extra material is available online you'll see this little Online Material logo in the sidebar.

Hint and tips

Other interesting bits and pieces will be explained in tip boxes like this one. Look out for them throughout the book.

Audio track

Online material

Each chapter in the book ends with a worksheet which will test you on the various concepts and musical ideas introduced in that chapter. Worksheet answers can be found on pages 159–167. Again, extra reference material and worksheets can be found on the website.

There's a huge amount of information packed into these pages, so our advice would be to take things slowly. If you spend about a week on each chapter that would be about right. Read through the text carefully and methodically, and listen to the online audio examples. Then try the worksheet at the end of the chapter, and visit **www.hybridpublications** to download other exercises. Only when you're sure that you've understood the concepts in one chapter should you move onto the next one. The information presented here builds incrementally – in other words each chapter builds on the one before it, so if you find yourself struggling go back to the previous chapter and re-read it.

Above all, we would urge you to take the ideas of music theory explored in these pages and apply them practically as a musician. Only by doing this will the real value and meaning of music theory become apparent.

Chapter 1:
The Minor Scale

Let's start by quickly revising what we already know about pitch. In 'How To Read Music' we discovered that in music notation pitch is written on a *stave*, consisting of five horizontal lines. At the beginning of the stave, we have a musical symbol called a *clef*, which defines which lines and spaces correspond to which pitches.

We looked at two clefs, the treble clef and the bass clef. Here they are again, with the note names marked underneath:

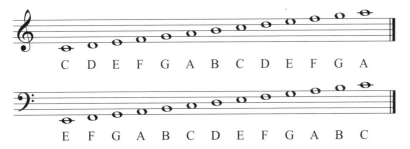

Remember that, for notes that fall either above or below the stave, we can extend the stave with shorter lines called *ledger lines*. In theory, these can be extended almost infinitely above or below the stave to add extra notes. In practice, however, we rarely use more than three or four ledger lines, as they can become very difficult to read. Notice that in the example above there is one note that falls between the treble and bass staves – it sits on the first ledger line above the bass stave, which is the same as the first ledger line below the treble stave. This note is known as Middle C because it's a C and you can find it in the middle of the two staves (it's also just about in the middle of most piano keyboards).

Accidentals

We also know that the basic pitches on the staves, which correspond to the letter names A–G (the white notes on the piano keyboard) can be altered by the use of *accidentals*. Accidentals is the collective term for *sharps* (♯), *flats* (♭), and *naturals* (♮) – signs that can be put in front of notes to alter their pitch by one semitone. Sharps

Jargon buster

Chromatic Scale
The full set of 12 pitches within one octave. From the Greek *chroma*, meaning colour.

The flat side

Note that the chromatic scale could also be written out using flats. So instead of C♯ we would write D♭ , instead of D♯ we'd have E♭, and so on.

raise the pitch of a note by one semitone, while flats *lower* the pitch by one semitone. Naturals just cancel out the effect of a sharp or flat, returning the note to its *natural* pitch. Using accidentals we can represent all 12 notes of the chromatic scale on the staves, like this:

Intervals

Interval is the word that musicians use to describe the distance between two pitches. An *octave* is probably the simplest interval to understand – it's the distance between two notes that share the same letter-name. So, if you start on the white note A on the piano and count up eight notes you'll get to another A, an octave higher.

When we include sharps and flats we find that there are 12 possible letter-names in the chromatic scale, which means that there are 12 possible intervals. Back in 'How To Read Music', we introduced these intervals and their musical names:

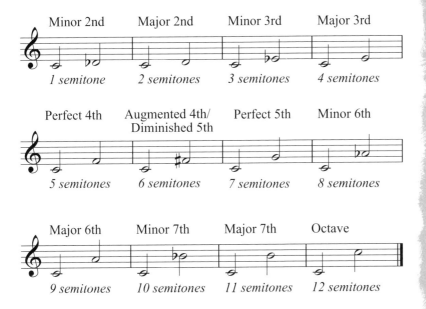

As you can see, each interval identifies two notes that are a specific number of semitones apart. There's one further interval that's not listed above, which identifies two notes of the same pitch (i.e. 0 semitones apart), which is called *unison*.

The major scale

Finally, I'm going to remind you about some very important collections of notes that are used in music, called *scales*. A scale is an ordered grouping of notes, in which some notes are more important than others. In particular, the note that the scale starts on (the *root note*) is considered to be particularly important.

We started by looking at the C major scale, and we noticed that it has a particular pattern of tones and semitones. This pattern is unique to the major scale and gives the scale its individual character. As we'll see, there are many different types of scale and each has a different pattern of tones and semitones. Overleaf you'll find a diagram showing the pattern of tones and semitones in the C major scale:

Going down!

Although all the intervals given here are *ascending* (i.e. the second note is higher than the first), there are also *descending* intervals, where the second note is lower than the first. The same names are used, though, so a note seven semitones lower than the previous note would be said to be a perfect fifth lower.

Online material

Visit **www.hybrid publications.com** for an interactive interval test.

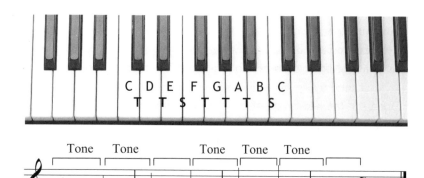

We also discovered that if we start the major scale on a different note, and apply the same pattern of tones and semitones, we will need to introduce sharps and flats to maintain the pattern. Here's what happens if we start the scale on G:

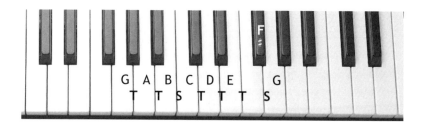

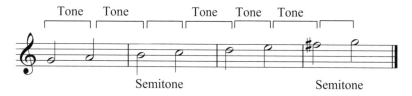

So, you'll see that in order to get the desired interval of a semitone between that last two notes of the scale, we need to introduce the note F♯. If we were to start the major scale on D, then we would find that we need to introduce the notes of F♯ and C♯. If we started on F, then we'd need to introduce the note of B♭, and so on.

Most music in the western world is built around scales, and frequently complete pieces or sections of larger works are constructed from one scale. When this happens we say that the piece is in a certain 'key'. From the notational point of view, this often means that we end up writing out a lot of accidentals. For example, for a piece in the key of D major, the chances are that nearly every F and C will need a sharp sign in front of them. So musicians invented a labour-saving device called a *key signature* – this is a group of sharps or flats that appears at the beginning of each stave. The exact grouping of notes is unique to each major key, and tells the musician to sharpen (or flatten) those notes every time that they occur.

A useful side-effect of this is that we can normally tell what key a piece of music is in, just by looking at the key signature. Here are the first three 'sharp' key signatures, which correspond to the keys of G major, D major and A major respectively:

And here are the first three 'flat' key signatures, which correspond to the keys of F major, B♭ major and E♭ major respectively:

Notice that key signatures can only contain sharps or flats, never both, and that they build up incrementally – the next key signature always includes the sharps or flats from the previous one, but adds one new one.

No naturals

Naturals don't appear in key signatures because they are only ever used to cancel out either a sharp or a flat.

There are a couple of handy tricks that can help you to identify the key of a piece from the key signature:
- In a sharp key signature, find the last sharp and go up one letter name. E.g. If the last sharp in the key signature is C♯, then the key is D major
- In a flat key signature, take off the last flat of the key signature to get the key of the piece. E.g. If the key signature has three flats, B♭, E♭ and A♭, take off the last one, A♭, to reveal the key of the piece, E♭ major.

15

From major to minor

We've already mentioned that music uses many different scales, and now it's time to introduce you to a new one – the minor scale. Just like the major scale, this scale has a specific pattern of tones and semitones, which gives it a unique character.

Let's start with the C major scale, as shown below:

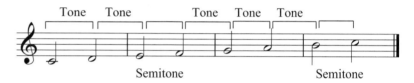

The C major scale starts and ends on C, but what would happen if we took exactly the same collection of notes, but started on A?

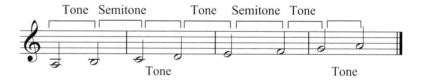

We've now created a different pattern of tones and semitones:

Tone–Semitone–Tone–Tone–Semitone–Tone–Tone

Listen to **Audio track 1** to hear what this sounds like. This is known as the *A natural minor scale* and, as we can see from the way in which we created it, it is very closely related to the C major scale. In fact, you might be forgiven for thinking that it is exactly the same as the C major scale, since it contains all the same notes. However, remember that scales are collections of notes in which some notes are more important than others. In the C major scale, the most important note is C; but in the A natural minor scale the most important note is A. When we listen to a piece in a minor key we hear everything in relation to this root note, and the effect on our ears is very different.

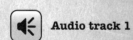

À la mode

The minor scale is actually a specific type of mode, called the *Aeolian mode*. Modes are created when we start a major scale on a note other than its root note. There are seven modes in total.

Audio track 1

Let's apply this pattern of tones and semitones to some more starting notes. Here's what happens if we start on E:

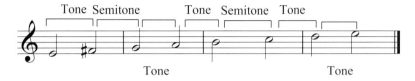

Note that, in order to get the opening interval of a tone, we've had to introduce an F♯. In fact, the scale of E natural minor contains exactly the same notes as the scale of G major, just as the scale of A natural minor contained exactly the same notes as C major.

Because the natural minor scale is basically the same as the major scale starting on its sixth degree, the major scale and the natural minor built on the sixth degree are are very closely related. In fact, E natural minor is said to be the *relative minor* of G major, and G major is said to be the *relative major* of E natural minor. Or, to put it another way, the third note of the natural minor scale will tell you the major scale with which it shares its collection of notes (and therefore its key signature).

Try the next example yourself and try to write out the scale of B natural minor.

Hint: find the relative major of B natural minor and use the same key signature.

Next, we're going to harmonise the natural minor scale and take a look at the chords that are created...

Two options

We can now see that each key signature can, in fact, represent one major key, or its relative minor. We can only decide which key the piece is in by examining the notes used to see whether the key is major or minor.

Answers

Answers to all exercises can be found at **www.hybrid publications.com**

Harmonising the natural minor scale

In 'How To Read Music' we harmonised the major scale by stacking thirds up on top of the original scale notes. We can do exactly the same thing with our new natural minor scale.

Let's look at A natural minor:

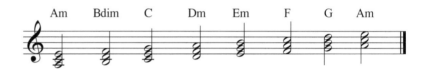

 Audio track 2

Listen to **Audio track 2** to hear what this sounds like. As we know, A natural minor contains exactly the same notes as C major, so it should be no surprise that harmonising the scale results in exactly the same set of chords: C major, D minor, E minor, F major, G major, A minor and B diminished. However, crucially, the chords occur in different places within the scale. So, for example the chord on the root note of the scale is A minor instead of C major:

Harmonised C major scale

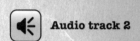 **Try this**

Experiment with harmonising other natural minor scales and compare the chords you generate with those from the harmonised relative major scale.

Harmonised A natural minor scale

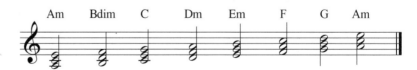

And on the fifth note of the scale, E, we find the chord of E minor, whereas in the harmonised C major scale, we had the chord of G major. The fact that the chord on the fifth degree is minor, rather than major has some rather inconvenient consequences, as we shall see...

The perfect cadence in major keys

Back in 'How To Read Music', we introduced the idea of *cadences*. These are specific combinations of chords that act like musical punctuation, showing us where phrases end. The most important cadence is known as a *Perfect Cadence*, and involves a move from a chord built on the fifth degree of the major scale (the *dominant*) to a chord built on the first degree of the scale (the *tonic*).

So, in C major a perfect cadence would look like this:

The dominant chord is often strengthened by the addition of the seventh degree of the scale on which it's built (in our example, an F natural). This is commonly referred to as a *dominant seventh*.

In C major the dominant seventh chord moving to the tonic chord looks like this (listen to **Audio track 3** to hear what it sounds like):

The dominant seventh chord contains the interval of an *augmented fourth* (in this case it's between the notes F and B). This is one of the most unstable and dissonant intervals in music – we hear it as wanting to move on to another, more stable chord.

In this cadence the notes F and B each only have to move by a semitone to E and C respectively, to reach the stable 'home' chord of C major. In addition, the top note (F) moves downwards, and the bottom note (B) moves upwards – this contrary motion is particularly satisfying.

*augmented
4th*

Audio track 3

Jargon buster

Contrary motion is where the upper and lower voices move in opposite directions.

The perfect cadence in minor keys

Now let's try to build a perfect cadence in A minor, the relative minor of C major. Let's take the 7th chord built on the fifth degree E, and move from there to the tonic chord, A minor:

Listen to **Audio track 4** to hear what this sounds like. While perfectly pleasing to the ear, this cadence doesn't have the definitive finality of the perfect cadence we heard in C major. This is because the V chord, Em7, doesn't contain that interval of an augmented fourth. If the chord were a major chord, E7, then we would have the augmented fourth interval between the notes of D and G♯.

So, why don't we just change the Em7 chord to E7, like this:

Notice that we have changed the G natural in the Em7 chord to a G♯ to create the chord of E7. Listen to **Audio track 5** to hear what this sounds like. It has all the finality of the major perfect cadence and sounds almost as satisfying. The only difference is that we end up on a minor chord instead of a major one, which means that the bottom note of the augmented fourth, the D, is moving down by a tone, to C, rather than a semitone, as it would in a major key.

So, by changing the G to a G♯ we were able to regain the power of the perfect cadence in a minor key. But how does this affect the natural minor scale – surely we can't just go around changing notes of the scale willy-nilly?

Audio track 4

Voice-leading

The voice-leading in this Em7–Am cadence isn't as satisfying as in our G7–C cadence. Although we still have contrary motion, both the D and G have to resolve by a tone instead of a semitone.

Audio track 5

The harmonic minor scale

Here's how A natural minor looks with G changed to a G♯:

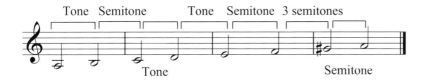

Listen to **Audio track 6** to hear what this sounds like. The addition of the G♯ may have helped with the perfect cadence but it has played havoc with our pattern of tones and semitones. Have a look at the pattern of intervals and compare it to our original A natural minor scale back on page 16.

The first difference comes between the sixth and seventh notes of the scale. Where we had an interval of a tone between F and G in the A natural minor scale, we now have a larger interval of three semitones between F and G♯. And where we previously had a tone between G and A, we now only have a semitone. Listen again to **Audio track 6** and look out for the distinctive effect created by these changes.

Musicians give this altered form of the natural minor scale a special name: the *harmonic minor scale*, so-called because it is created out of the harmonic necessity of having a major chord on the fifth degree of the scale.

So, to convert any natural minor scale to a harmonic minor scale, all you need to do is to take the 7th note of the scale and sharpen it (i.e. move it up by one semitone). Here's the scale of E harmonic minor:

Audio track 6

Going egyptian

This larger gap between the sixth and seventh degrees gives a distinctive sound, which is sometimes used to to denote 'Egyptian' or Oriental music.

Have a go yourself. Here's the scale of G natural minor – underneath, write out the scale of G harmonic minor.

For even more of a challenge, try this exercise. Here is the scale of F major. On the stave below, write out the relative natural minor scale, then, on the stave below that, write out the harmonic minor version:

The melodic minor scale

We're going to conclude this chapter with a look at a very strange scale, called the *melodic minor scale*. It's strange because it is a very rare example of a scale that is different on the way up and the way down.

The harmonic minor scale is, as its name suggests, great for harmony – it gives us lovely strong perfect cadences. But that interval of three semitones between the sixth and seventh degrees of the scale is a real problem when it comes to melody. Just try singing up and down the scale and you'll see what I mean – it's a very tricky interval to get right. What we need is something that combines the sharpened seventh note of the harmonic minor scale, but which smooths out that ungainly jump.

Step forward the melodic minor scale. On the way up, we sharpen both the sixth and seventh degrees, reducing the gap between them to a tone:

And on the way down we simply use the natural minor pattern:

Hey presto! We have the best of both worlds. Listen to **Audio track 7** to hear what this scale sounds like. All three forms of the minor scale are in regular use in many different styles of music, from western classical music, through to Latin music, folk music from around the world, and soul, rock and pop music.

Audio track 7

Worksheet 1 (answers on page 159)

1. Write out the scales of F major (on the treble stave below) and E major (on the bass stave below). Don't use a key signature – use accidentals where necessary:

2. Write out the scales of G natural minor (on the bass stave below) and F natural minor (on the treble stave below). Don't use a key signature – use accidentals where necessary:

3. Write out the scales of B harmonic minor (on the bass stave below) and D harmonic minor (on the treble stave below). Don't use a key signature – use accidentals where necessary:

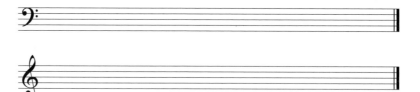

Chapter 2: Key Signatures

So, we've seen how the pattern of tones and semitones in the major scale gives rise to the need for key signatures. When we build a major scale starting on G, we need to add the F♯, and when we build a major scale starting on D, we need to add both an F♯ and a C♯.

If we look closely at the relationship between the root note of a major scale and the number of sharps in its key signature we might start to notice a pattern. C major has no sharps, G major has one sharp and D major has two sharps. Let's plot these notes on the keyboard:

Spot the pattern

Patterns are everywhere in music, from rhythmic patterns to harmonic ones. This is one of the reasons that maths and music are said to be very closely related.

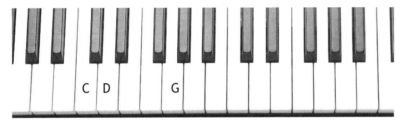

No obvious pattern, yet; but let's see what happens if we move the D note up an octave:

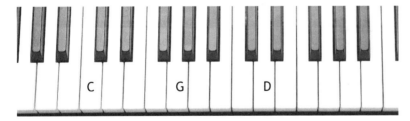

Now we can see very clearly that the G is an interval of a fifth above C, and D is a fifth above G. This seems to suggest that if we go up a fifth from D, to A, and construct a major scale on that note, we might find a key signature with three sharps. Let's try it:

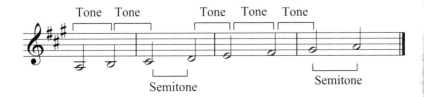

So, every time we move the root note of the scale up by a fifth we add one sharp to the key signature. If we move up a fifth from A to E, we add another sharp, giving a key signature with four sharps:

And so on; B major has five sharps and F♯ major has six. Here are the first six sharp key signatures in full:

G major   D major   A major   E major   B major   F♯ major

Flat key signatures

There's a very similar pattern for flat key signatures. As we've seen already F major has a key signature of one flat while B♭ major has a key signature of two flats. Plotting these on the keyboard looks like this:

Here we can clearly see that to get from C to F we have to move up by an interval of a fourth, and that we then move up by another interval of a fourth to get to the B♭ note.

But there's another way of looking at this pattern. This time, let's put the C note at the top of the keyboard and find the F below it, and the B♭ below that:

We're starting to see that the interval of a fifth is extremely important in music theory. Remember that the root movement of a fifth in the perfect cadence is one of the reasons for its power.

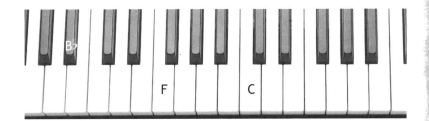

Now we can clearly see that F is a fifth *below* C, and B♭ is a fifth *below* F. There's a pleasing symmetry to this pattern; for sharp keys, we go *up* a fifth to find the next sharp key signature, while for flat keys, we go *down* a fifth. Using this method, you'll quickly find that the first six flat key signatures belong to the keys of F, B♭, E♭, A♭, D♭ and G♭ major. But hang on a minute – G♭ is the same note as F♯, isn't it? How can the same note have two different key signatures?

G♭ and F# are known as enharmonic equivalents – in other words they are different names for the same note. A piece in F♯ major could just as easily be written in G♭ major – it would sound exactly the same.

The circle of fifths

As we've seen, the interval of a fifth is very important when it comes to relating different keys to one another. We can plot all of these key signature on a diagram that musicians call the 'circle of fifths':

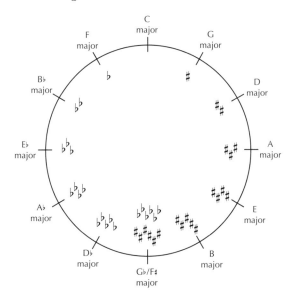

Inversions

Moving up by a fifth and moving down by a fourth will reach the same note, an octave apart. The interval of a fourth is therefore said to be the *inversion* of a fifth. Any interval can be inverted by subtracting it from 9: so the inversion of a 2nd is a 7th, and so on.

Online material

Visit **www.hybrid publications.com** for a reference sheet on inversions and an interactive test.

So, to get from one sharp key signature to the next we go round the circle of fifths clockwise, with each stop on the journey representing an upwards jump of a fifth. Going anti-clockwise takes us from one flat key signature to the next, with each stop representing a downwards jump of a fifth.

We start at C, which has a key signature of no sharps or flats, and depending on whether we move round the 'flat side' or the 'sharp side' of the circle, we end up on the opposite site at G♭ or F♯, which, as we've seen, are the same note.

The 12 'stops' around the circle cover all 12 notes of the chromatic scale and therefore cover every possible key signature. In theory we could continue anti-clockwise from G♭ to create key signatures with more than six flats, but in practice this creates key signatures that are overly large and unwieldy, so they tend not to be used. Similarly, we could continue round the circle of fifths in a clockwise motion, adding more and more sharps beyond the six required for F♯ major, but in practice this is never done.

Some good news

You now know all 12 major key signatures. But what about the minor scales that we looked at in Chapter 1?

Well, you may remember that back in the previous chapter we introduced the concept of a *relative minor*; A minor is the relative minor of C major for example, and, crucially, *shares the same key signature*. So, if you know the key signatures for all 12 major keys, you also automatically know the key signatures for all 12 of their relative minors.

So, for example, if you want to know the key signature for B minor, simply figure out its relative major, by counting up three steps in the scale – B to C♯ to D – to get the relative major of D major, and use that key signature: two sharps. Similarly, for F♯ minor, count up three steps to A – key signature, three sharps.

Learn the cycle

If you play a harmony instrument like piano or guitar, a good exercise is to practise playing all the way around the circle of fifths. Start at one of the 'stops' on the circle and play chords a fifth apart until you land back on the chord you started on.

Here's how the circle of fifths looks for minor keys:

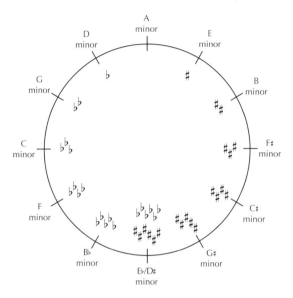

Add it up

Compare this diagram with the one on page 27 and note that each major 'stop' on the cycle has been replaced with its relative minor.

Test yourself

Look at the following key signatures. Write the major keys that they correspond to under the stave – we've done the first one for you:

B♭ major

Answers

Answers to all these exercises can be found at **www.hybrid publications.com**

For these key signatures, write the *minor* keys to which they relate underneath:

Now do the opposite; write the correct key signature for each key onto the stave below:

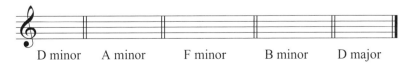

D minor   A minor   F minor   B minor   D major

Hints & tips

Check back to page 15 to remind yourself of the shortcuts for identifying keys from key signatures.

Enharmonic equivalents

When we discussed the circle of fifths we introduced the idea that one note could have more than one name – F♯ and G♭, for example. Surely music theory is confusing enough already without having several names for the same thing?

As it happens, enharmonic equivalents, at these notes are called, can come in very handy. To discover why, let's start by looking at the scale of F♯ minor.

As we know, we can figure out the key signature for F♯ minor by simply moving up three letter names to its relative major: A. Looking back at the circle of fifths we can see that A has three sharps. So let's start by creating a stave with three sharps:

Let's continue by writing out the scale of F♯ natural minor. As we saw back in Chapter 1, the natural minor contains exactly the same notes as its relative major. Since we have already added the key signature, we won't need any further accidentals and we can just write out the scale starting on F♯, like this:

Now let's convert this scale into a *harmonic* minor scale. As you'll remember from Chapter 1, we do this by simply sharpening the seventh note of the scale.

At the moment the seventh note of the scale is E, so if we sharpen that note we will create an F. If we write out the scale with this alteration it looks like this:

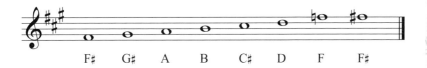

F♯   G♯   A   B   C♯   D   F   F♯

This looks a little odd, doesn't it? There's a jump between the D and F natural, which looks strange, but what's more disconcerting is that there are two notes that use the letter name F, and none that uses the letter name E. Up to this point every scale we've looked at has used each one of the letter names from A to G once, and once only.

Having two different Fs – an F natural and an F sharp – complicates life, because, apart from anything else, the key signature tells us that every F should be sharpened, so every time we want to use the sharpened seventh degree of the scale we'll have to introduce an accidental to spell out F natural.

We could solve all these problems at a stroke if, instead of sharpening the E to F natural, we just called it E♯. Now, we use each letter only once, and there's no ungainly gap:

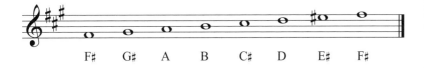

F♯   G♯   A   B   C♯   D   E♯   F♯

Remember, this scale sounds exactly the same as the scale that's written out at the top of the page – changing the F to an E♯ (its enharmonic equivalent) is just for notational neatness, it has absolutely no effect on the sound that we hear. Enharmonic equivalents only appear in some scales, and despite the fact that they seem to complicate things, as we explore the world of music theory in more depth, you'll find that they are actually extremely helpful.

Let's look at another scale that uses an enharmonic equivalent, C♯ minor. Here's the scale of C♯ natural minor – remember, count up three notes to get the relative major, in this case, E, and then use the key signature for that major key:

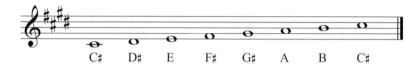

C♯   D♯   E   F♯   G♯   A   B   C♯

Stay sharp

Harmonic minor scales often need to use enharmonic equivalents because of the presence of the sharpened seventh degree.

Now let's convert this natural minor scale into a harmonic minor scale by sharpening the seventh note. The seventh note is currently a B; if we sharpen this to a C we will run into the same problems that we found in the F♯ harmonic minor scale, so let's use B♯ instead:

C♯   D♯   E   F♯   G♯   A   B♯   C♯

Voilà! Another triumph for the enharmonic equivalent.

There's just one more trick that we can use when writing out harmonic minor scales, and again, it's used to keep notation looking neat and to maintain our system of every scale including each letter name only once. Let's start by looking at the scale of G♯ natural minor.

The relative major of G♯ minor is B, so we'll start with the key signature of B major, five sharps:

And here is our scale of G♯ natural minor:

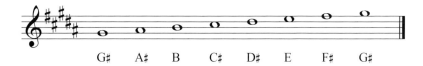

As we did before, we now want to turn this natural minor scale into a harmonic minor scale, by sharpening the seventh note.

But this is where we run into a problem. The seventh note of the scale is F♯ – it's already a sharp note. We could sharpen it to G natural, but then we run into the problem of having two G letter names and no F in the scale.

The solution is simplicity itself, we just add *another* sharp to the existing sharp, turning F♯ into F♯♯, or F *double sharp*. So now the scale looks like this:

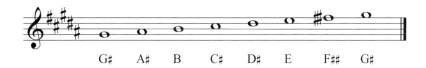

So, honour is satisfied – we have included all seven letter names in the scale. There's just one final tweak; having those two sharp signs next to each other looks a bit messy, so we use a separate sign for a double sharp, which looks like this: ✕ .

So, here's the final correct scale of G♯ harmonic minor:

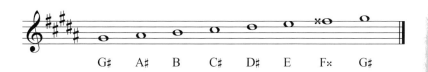

Don't panic!

You'll be relieved to hear that there is no such thing as triple sharps!

Double sharps and double flats

With music notation being the logical system that it is, it would be reasonable to assume that if we have created the concept of the 'double sharp' then we might also need to create the concept of a 'double flat'. And indeed this turns out to be the case. However, unlike the double sharp, there's no special symbol for the double flat, it's just written as ♭♭. Here are some examples of enharmonic equivalents using double flats:

Now have a go yourself. On the stave below are written various double sharp and double flat notes – next to each one write its enharmonic equivalent without the use of accidentals.

Answers

Answers to these exercises can be found at **www.hybrid publications.com**

Now let's do the reverse; try writing enharmonic equivalents of the following notes using double sharps:

And now with double flats:

Cancelling double sharps and flats

As with ordinary accidentals, double sharps and flats only take effect for one bar. But what do we do if we want to cancel them within the same bar?

Let's look at C✗, for example. If we want to cancel the double sharp completely, so that the second note is a C natural, we can use a normal natural sign:

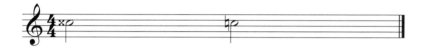

However, this is an unusual musical situation; what you are more likely to find is a situation where a C♯ is sharpened to C✗, and then returns to C♯. In this case, we use a natural and sharp sign together, to indicate that the double sharp has been cancelled but that the note retains its original single sharp, like this:

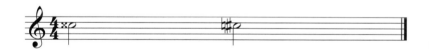

The same applies when cancelling a double flat; a single natural sign will cancel the double flat completely, and a natural sign and flat sign together will return the note to a single flat:

Micro-sharps

In some musical styles, which use microtones (intervals smaller than a semitone), there are special symbols for half-sharps and three-quarter-sharps.

Major and minor key signatures

Online material

Visit
www.hybrid publications.com
for a reference sheet on major scales.

For reference, here are the 12 major scales:

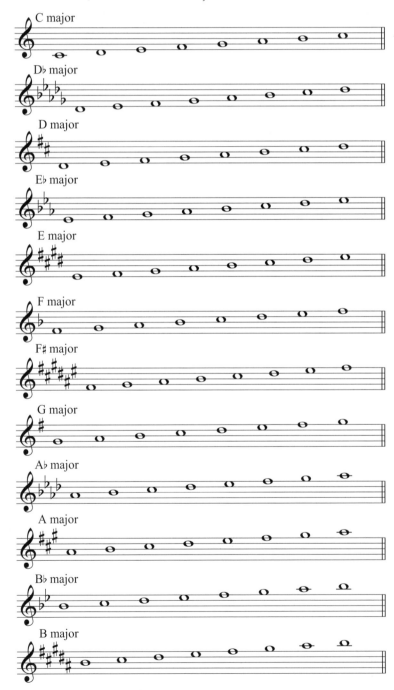

Test yourself

Try writing down all 12 key signatures on 12 pieces of paper and put them in a bowl. In another bowl put three bits of paper with the words 'major', 'minor' and 'harmonic' written on them. Take one piece of paper from each bowl, randomly, and see if you can write out the relevant scale in that key signature.

Here are the 12 melodic minor scales – harmonic minor with a sharpened sixth on the way up, natural minor on the way down:

 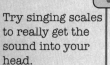
Hints & tips

Try singing scales to really get the sound into your head.

Worksheet 2 (answers on page 160)

1. Write out the scales of E♭ major (on the treble stave below) and B major (on the bass stave below). Use the correct key signatures in each case.

Answers

Answers to this worksheet can be found on page 160.

2. Write out the scales of F harmonic minor (on the treble stave below) and C harmonic minor (on the bass stave below). Use the correct key signatures in each case.

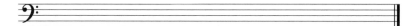

Online material

Additional worksheets are available at **www.hybrid publications.com.**

3. Various double sharps and double flats are written on the stave below – next to each one write its enharmonic equivalent without the use of accidentals.

4. Write enharmonic equivalents of the following notes using double sharps:

Chapter 3: Rhythm

We covered the basis of rhythmic notation back in 'How To Read Music', but let's have a quick refresher here. By starting with the semibreve and repeatedly halving it, we create a range of note values, from the minim all the way down to the semiquaver.

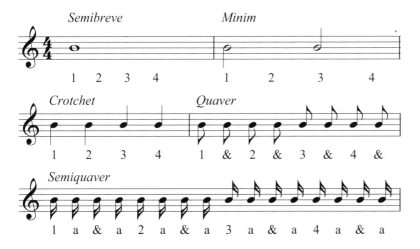

Not only that, but we discovered that for every note value that tells you how long to play a note for, there is an equivalent symbol, called a *rest*, which tells you how long to remain silent. Here's a reminder of the note values and their corresponding rests:

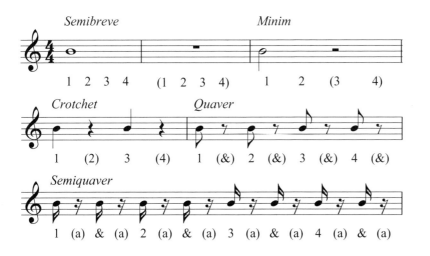

UK vs. US

The names used here for note values are UK terms. The US equivalents are (from long to short): whole note, half note, quarter note, eighth note and sixteenth note.

We also learned that these basic note values can be altered by the use of *dots* and *ties*.

Ties are curved lines that join two notes together. They tell us that instead of playing two individual notes, we should play one note that lasts as long as the two note values added together. So, for example, if we wanted to notate a note that lasted for three and a half beats, we could do it like this:

A dot placed after a note increases the length of that note by 50% (not to be confused with a dot above or below the note, which is an indication to play *staccato*, or detached). Dots are a more efficient way of writing some note values, but they aren't as versatile as ties. Here are some simple tied rhythms that can be converted into dotted rhythms:

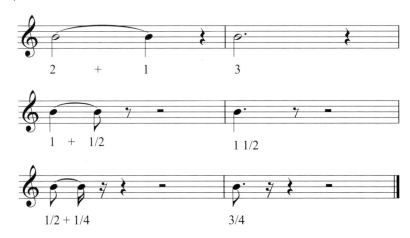

Finally, note that ties can be used across barlines whereas dotted notes are only used within the bar. Rests, of course, don't require ties, since there is no sound to be continued, although dots are used to simplify and reduce the number of rests where possible.

The full set of note values

The note and rest values that you already know will be sufficient for nearly all musical situations you are likely to encounter. But for the sake of completeness, there are two more note values that you should be familiar with. These exist at the extreme ends of the range of note values – one is very short and one is very long.

Let's start at the short end of the spectrum, with the demisemi-quaver. As its name suggests, this note value can be created by dividing the semiquaver in half, creating a note value of an eighth of a beat.

The demisemiquaver looks just like the semiquaver, except that it has an extra tail, making a total of three tails (or three beams if the demisemiquavers are beamed together, as they usually are). In fact, there's nothing to stop you adding more and more beams or tails to create shorter and shorter notes, although the practical use of such note values is negligible. For example, a note with four tails or beams is known as a hemidemisemiquaver and lasts for one sixteenth of a beat.

Similarly, the demisemiquaver rest is like the semiquaver rest, but with an additional bar, like this:

You're most likely to encounter demisemiquavers in a very slow tempo, or when notating ornaments (more on this in Chapter 9).

Even shorter!

There is an even shorter note than the hemidemisemi-quaver, which is half as long, and rejoices in the name of semihemidemi-semiquaver.

The breve

At the other end of the note value spectrum, we find the *breve*. Given that we already know a note value called the semibreve, it would be reasonable to guess that the breve should be twice as long. And indeed it is, being the equivalent of eight crotchet beats.

Confusingly, the breve can be written in two different ways. Option one is a note that looks very similar to the semibreve, with the addition of two small vertical lines on either side. Option two is a more rectangular note head with slight vertical extensions:

We haven't yet encountered a bar which could accommodate a breve. A bar of 4/4, for example, will be completely filled by one semibreve, so a breve would be two times too long to fit in. However, using our knowledge of time signatures we can imagine a musical situation in which a breve might be required...

Remember that in a time signature the top note tells us the number of beats in the bar, while the bottom note tells us the note value of each beat. So in 3/4, for example, we have three crotchet beats per bar, while in 6/8 we have six quaver beats. Notice that the bigger the bottom number, the shorter the note value of the beat; conversely, the lower the bottom number, the longer the note value of the beat.

So, if we were to create a time signature of 4/2, for example, this would have four minim beats per bar. Hey presto, we now have a bar long enough to accommodate the breve, like this:

Full bar's rest

Also note the breve rest, which fills the space between the two stave lines completely. The breve is rare in modern scores, but can be found more frequently in notation from the Baroque and Renaissance eras of music.

4/2 is the only time signature in which the breve rest is used to denote a whole bar's rest. In all other time signatures a semibreve rest can be used to show a complete bar's rest.

Try these exercises to make sure that you have understood the breve and demisemiquaver note values. Start by replacing the rests in this rhythm with groups of demisemiquavers:

Answers

Answers to all these exercises can be found at **www.hybrid publications.com**

Now try writing out the first two bars of this example in the third bar, doubling the speed of every note:

Finally, try writing out the first two bars of this example again, doubling every note value:

Triplets

Back in 'How To Read Music' we covered the basic concept of triplets, but let's have a quick recap here. Basically, triplets are three notes squeezed into the time of two. In other words, these groups of triplet quavers tells us to play three notes in the time of two quavers:

Confused?

To avoid any confusion some composers write tuplets as a ratio, like this: 5:4. This indicates that five notes are to be played in the time of four.

An ordinary quaver would last for half a beat, allowing two to be played during one beat. The triplet quavers only last for a third of a beat each, allowing three to be played during one beat.

As we saw, triplets can be applied to any note value – minims, crotchets, semiquavers, or any other value – and they are always interpreted in this way. In fact, this concept of playing a certain number of notes 'in the time of' a number of other notes can be extended beyond groups of three; these groupings of notes are called *tuplets*.

The triplets shown above use only one note value – three quavers in the time of two, for example. However, within this overall grouping we can combine notes to form longer note values, as long as the overall value of the triplet stays the same. So for example, we can have a crotchet-quaver triplet, or a quaver-crotchet triplet:

The basic principle still applies though: the overall total note value of three quavers has to be played in the time of two quavers. So the crotchet under the triplet bracket lasts for two thirds of a beat, while the quaver lasts for a third of a beat, giving a total duration of one beat.

Similarly, we can substitute any of the notes in the triplet for rests, again as long as the total value of the triplet still adds up to a multiple of three. So, we can use triplet groupings like this:

Listen to **Audio track 8** to hear what this sounds like. Try these exercises to practise your triplets. Start by filling in the gaps in this rhythm (marked with an asterisk) with groups of quaver triplets:

Audio track 8

Now try the same exercise but using a mixture of note values and rests in each triplet. There are a variety of ways of doing this – we've given one possible answer on the website.

Answers

Answers to all these exercises can be found at **www.hybrid publications.com**

Duplets

As we saw in 'How To Read Music', there is a close connection between triplets in simple time signatures like 4/4, 3/4 and 2/4 and compound time signatures like 12/8, 9/8 and 6/8. This is because in a compound time signature each beat is broken down into subdivisions of three, which is exactly what we are doing with triplets in simple time signatures, where the beat is subdivided into twos.

Hopefully, you should be gradually realising that music theory is supremely logical and we're about to see another example of this. If we have a symbol that allows us to play three notes in time signatures where the beat is subdivided into two, it should also be possible to have a symbol that allows us to play two notes in the time of three, in time signatures where the beat is subdivided into three.

And sure enough, such a symbol exists – it's called a *duplet*. Imagine a bar of 6/8, filled with two groups of three quavers:

Now, suppose that we wanted to play groups of two quavers instead of three – we'd write it like this:

Listen to **Audio track 9** to hear the first example followed by the second. The duplet tells us to play the two quavers in the time of three. (An alternative way of notating this would simply be to add a dot after each of the two quavers.) Like triplets, duplets can be applied to any note value, and can include rests. However, you can't mix note values within one duplet, because, by definition, in a group of two even notes, both notes must be the same duration. Of course, the example above could just as easily be written out in a 2/4 time signature, like this:

Both examples will sound exactly the same; the choice of style of notation will depend upon the prevailing rhythmic subdivision of the piece – if the overall feel is in threes then duplets will be used, whereas if most of the piece features beat subdivisions in twos, then the 2/4 option will be preferred, using triplets where necessary.

Let's try a couple of exercises to reinforce the differences and similarities between triplets and duplets. Firstly, try writing out this example in 12/8 in 4/4:

Now let's do the opposite: here's a rhythm in 3/4 – try writing it out in 9/8 using duplets where necessary:

And now try using dotted notes instead of duplets:

Answers

Answers to all these exercises can be found at **www.hybrid publications.com**

Rhythm notation – summary

We've now covered all the elements of notation that describe rhythm. For handy reference, they are all presented in brief on these two pages, starting with note and rest values:

Remember that both dots and ties can be used to create further note values from all of the above.

Here is a summary of the simple and compound time signatures:

Hints & tips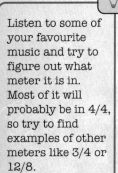

Listen to some of your favourite music and try to figure out what meter it is in. Most of it will probably be in 4/4, so try to find examples of other meters like 3/4 or 12/8.

And finally, here are examples of various tuplets and duplets in simple and compound time signatures:

Worksheet 3 (answers on page 161)

1. Try writing this example in 4/4 again in 2/4, doubling the speed of every note:

2. Try writing this example in 4/4 again in 4/2, halving the speed of every note:

3. Write out this example in 12/8 in 4/4, using triplets where necessary:

4. How many demisemiquavers could be fitted into one breve?

Chapter 4: Clefs

In 'How To Read Music' we introduced the concept of the stave as a grid on which we can plot pitches, as well as the idea of a clef, which sits at the beginning of the stave and defines exactly where on the 'pitch continuum' we are. It does this by specifying the pitch of one line on the stave, from which the others can then be derived.

We dealt almost exclusively with two clefs, the treble clef and the bass clef. Here are the notes on the treble clef:

C D E F G A B C D E F G A

And here are the notes on the bass clef:

E F G A B C D E F G A B C

And here are these note ranges illustrated on the piano keyboard:

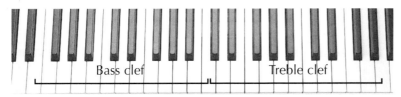

Bass clef   Treble clef

Notice that the two clefs define distinct and separate ranges of notes; notice too that there are notes above, below, and *between* these two ranges that are not covered by the pitches notated above.

One way that we can extend the range of notes covered by a clef is to use ledger lines – small additional lines that extend above and below the stave, and on which extra notes can be plotted.

Jargon buster

Pitch continuum just means the complete range of possible musical notes, from low to high.

Other names

Remember that the treble clef is sometimes also called the 'G clef', and the bass clef is sometimes called the 'F clef', because those are the notes that each clef defines on the stave. Strictly speaking, they are actually only *examples* of G and F clefs respectively, as other types do exist.

Using octaves

Sometimes if we want to notate an entire passage to be played much higher or lower than the stave, we can write it out on the stave and then use an '8va' or '8vb' indication to show that the entire passage should be played either an octave higher or lower. Sometimes the word 'loco' is used after such an indication to show that the octave transposition has come to an end.

Here's the treble clef with three ledger lines above and below the stave:

F G A B C D E F G A B C D E F G A B C D E

In theory, we can go on adding ledger lines indefinitely, but in practice this isn't done as they can become very difficult to read (and as we're about to see there are other better ways to represent pitches that fall outside the stave.) Here's the bass clef with three ledger lines above and below the stave:

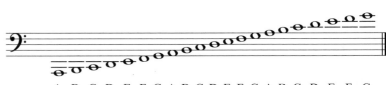

A B C D E F G A B C D E F G A B C D E F G

Again, here are these two note ranges plotted on the piano keyboard:

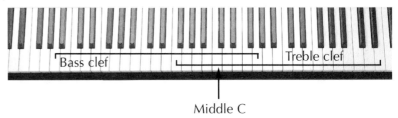

Middle C

This time notice that the two ranges *overlap* in the middle. What this means is that there is a group of notes (from middle C to the G above) that appear on both staves. This is an important principle – *the same pitch can appear in different places on different staves*.

Think of a stave as a 'window' through which we can see a certain portion of a continuum of pitches, which extends higher and lower at either extreme. If we look through a different 'window' we see a different portion of this continuum, which might or might not cross over with the range that we saw from a different 'window'.

As the names of the treble and bass staves suggest, they developed through a need to notate vocal music. The treble clef is a convenient way of notating the range of the treble [unbroken, boy's] voice, while the bass clef conveniently covers the range of the bass register.

Armed with this bit of historical knowledge, you might reasonably ask if other clefs were developed to notate conveniently other voice types – what about alto and tenor, for example? Sure enough, alto and tenor clefs do exist for this very reason, and, although they are used much less often than the treble and bass clefs, it is still worthwhile familiarising yourself with them.

The alto clef

Let's start with the alto clef. The clef looks like an ornate letter B, with a central arrow pointing at the middle line of the clef.

Somewhat confusingly, given its similarity to the letter B, the alto clef is called a 'C clef', because the central arrow gives the location of the note middle C on the stave. Knowing this bit of information we can now plot pitches on the stave, and find the corresponding range covered by the clef on the piano keyboard.

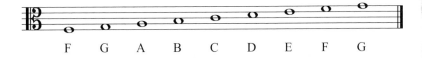

F   G   A   B   C   D   E   F   G

Alto clef

Using the alto

The most common use for the alto clef is to notate music for the viola (which also uses the treble clef for its upper register).

Top tip

A quick rule of thumb when reading from the alto clef is to read as if reading from the treble clef, but transpose up a letter-name and down an octave. It's easier than it sounds!

Answers

Answers to these exercises can be found at
www.hybrid publications.com

Note that the range of notes covered by the alto clef corresponds very closely to the range of overlapping notes that is created by using three ledger lines in the treble and bass clefs. In other words, the alto clef is a convenient way of representing those notes without using ledger lines. Take a look at the ranges of notes represented by the treble, alto and bass clefs

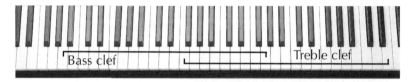

Alto clef (no ledger lines)

Try these exercises to test your knowledge of the alto clef. First, write these notes on the stave (remember that some notes can be found in two places on the stave):

Now, write the letter names of these notes under the stave:

Finally, try writing out this melody, given on the treble stave, on the alto stave:

The tenor clef

To complete our 'quartet' of clefs all that remains is for us to look at the tenor clef. As we've discovered this clef developed in order to represent the range of the tenor voice, which lies between alto and bass. Slightly confusingly, the tenor clef is exactly the same shape as the alto clef (resembling an ornate letter B), but is positioned slightly differently on the stave:

Note that this time the central 'arrow' is pointing to the second stave line from the top, showing that this line represents middle C. Notice too that the whole clef juts out a little bit above the stave:

D   E   F   G   A   B   C   D   E

Tenor clef (no ledger lines)

Other clefs

Historically, many other clefs have been used, but nearly all have now fallen by the wayside, including the baritone, mezzo-soprano and soprano clefs.

Contrast this with the alto clef, which points to the middle line of the stave, and sits entirely within the stave.

The tenor clef is still used today, by cellos, bassoons and tenor trombones, although all of these instruments also use the bass clef. Ironically, like the alto clef, it is not used by singers. Tenor singers use a mixture of the bass and treble clefs.

Here are the ranges for all four clefs, shown on the piano keyboard:

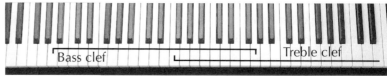

Tenor clef (no ledger lines)

Alto clef (no ledger lines)

Now let's try some exercises to practise the tenor clef. First, write the letter names of these notes under the stave:

Next, write these notes on the tenor stave:

B   C   E   G   F   A

Now try writing out this melody, currently notated in the alto clef, in the tenor clef:

 Answers

Answers to these exercises can be found at **www.hybrid publications.com**

Tips and tricks

If you're ever confronted with a score that uses the alto clef, here's a trick that you can use quickly to figure out what's what.

As we've seen, middle C on the alto clef is found on the middle line. Compare this with the treble clef, where the C above middle C is found in the space above the middle line:

 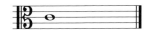

So, a shortcut to playing from the alto clef is to imagine that you are reading from the treble clef down an octave and up one note. So, for example, here's a simple phrase in the alto clef:

Imagine you're reading this in the treble clef and transpose it up one ledger line as you read, which will give this:

Now play down the octave:

This requires some mental gymnastics at first, but with practice you'll find that you can do it very quickly. You can do a very similar trick with the tenor clef – this time, imagine that you are reading from the treble clef, but *down* one note and an octave.

The family of clefs

Let's summarise the four clefs that we now know.

Treble clef
Used for: soprano & alto voices, right hand of piano music, violin, flute, clarinet, oboe, trumpet, horn, guitar, etc.

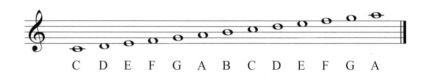

C D E F G A B C D E F G A

Alto clef
Used for: viola

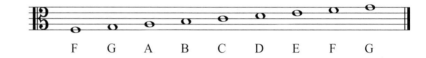

F G A B C D E F G

Tenor clef
Used for: 'cello, bassoon, tenor trombone

D E F G A B C D E

Bass clef
Used for: tenor & bass voice, left hand of piano music, 'cello, double bass, bassoon, trombone, tuba etc.

E F G A B C D E F G A B C

To really test your knowledge of clefs, try these exercises. First, try writing these notes on the alto and tenor clefs:

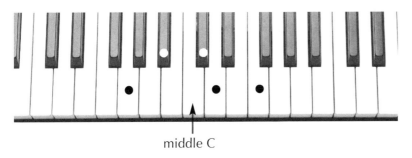

middle C

Short score and open score

We've seen in this chapter how the different vocal ranges of the human voice force us to find ways of notating different pitches. Conventionally, there are four main voice types: soprano, alto, tenor and bass, and their ranges are roughly as follows:

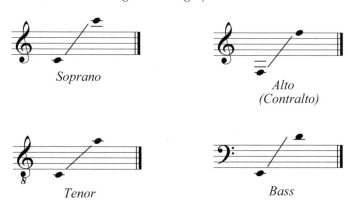

Everyone's voice is different, of course, but these divisions are useful rules of thumb for singers and composers. When writing music for these four voice types together (known as SATB – Soprano, Alto, Tenor, Bass) we have a couple of options. The first is to simply use one stave per voice, which is known as *open score*:

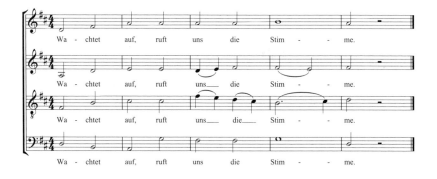

Note that the tenor line is written in the treble clef, but that the clef has an extra '8' below it – this means that everything on that stave should be sung an octave lower.

Open score is a very clear way of writing, but it takes up a lot of space and it can be difficult to see, in one glance, exactly what the harmony is doing. So, we have another option, which is known as *short score*. In this format, the soprano and alto voices are written on one treble stave, and the tenor and bass voices are combined on one bass stave, like this:

The soprano part is written with its stems upwards, while the alto part's notes all have their stems pointing downwards. Similarly, in the bass clef the tenor part's stems are pointing upwards while the bass part's stems point downwards. If the soprano and alto (or tenor and bass) sing the same note then one notehead is used, with both up- and down-stems.

As you can see from the example above, the fact that the stem direction is used to indicate which voice is which means that rules about stem direction are ignored. So, for example, on the treble clef you will find notes above the central line that have stems going upwards; conversely, you will also find notes below the central line that have stems pointing downwards.

If the parts cross over, so that the soprano is singing a lower note than the alto, for example, the soprano stem should still point upwards and the alto stem should still point downwards.

Notice too that the tenor part is written differently in the short score format. Here is it written at the sounding pitch, on the bass clef, whereas in the open score format it is written an octave higher than it sounds, on the treble clef.

Upper or lower?

When we write more than one part on one stave in this way we use the term 'voice' to distinguish between the two. The part with stems upward is called the 'upper voice' and the part with stems downward is called the 'lower voice'. These names are still used even if the lines in question are instruments rather than vocal parts.

Worksheet 4 (answers on page 162)

1. Write the letter names of these notes under the stave:

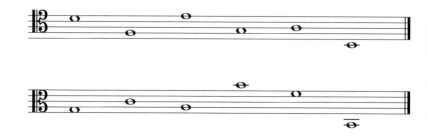

2. Write these notes on the Alto and Tenor staves below, using up to one ledger line. Remember that some notes can be found in more than one place:

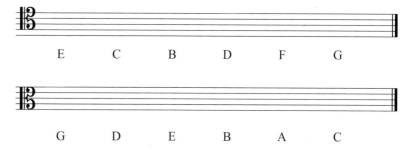

3. Copy this passage into the bass clef:

4. Which clef is used mainly by the viola?

Chapter 5: Transposing

I this chapter we're going to look at a musical technique called *transposition*. This simply means taking a passage of music and moving it higher or lower, while maintaining the pattern of intervals so that the shape and sound of the melody remains the same.

There are many reasons why we might want to do this; for example, a singer might find that a certain melody is too high for his or her vocal range, and that it needs to be transposed downwards to be more comfortable. Or perhaps we might want to arrange a melody for a bass instrument, like the bassoon, that was originally written for a much higher instrument, like the flute – again, we will need to transpose the piece down in order to make it playable.

The simplest form of transposition is to move a musical extract up or down by an octave. The key of the extract and the letter names of all the notes will remain the same. Here, we've taken a melody in the treble clef and transposed it up an octave:

We've achieved this by taking each note and moving it up by an octave – we have to apply exactly the same transposition to every note in the melody, otherwise the intervals between successive notes will be changed, and the shape and sound of the melody will be altered. Note that the key signature has stayed the same, as have the letter names of the individual notes. Listen to **Audio track 10** to hear the difference between the two versions.

Just the pitch

Don't forget that transposition only affects the pitch of notes. All the rhythms, dynamics, articulation and phrase marks etc. will stay exactly the same.

Audio track 10

Don't fall into the trap of thinking that writing out a melody in a different clef is the same thing as transposition. Sometimes we can use a different clef once we have transposed something because it is substantially higher or lower than the original melody, but equally, we can also write out exactly the same section of music in two different clefs without transposing it at all. Here's an example of the same phrase written in treble and alto clefs:

There has been no transposition here – these are simply two different ways of notating the same thing. However, this example shows a melody that has been transposed down by an octave, and written in the bass clef:

To keep the transposed version of this melody in the treble clef would have involved an unacceptable number of ledger lines, so the bass clef has been used to make the music easier to read.

Cheating?

Modern music notation programs such as *Sibelius* and *Finale* can transpose passages at the click of a button. But it's no substitute for learning how to do it yourself. Honest.

Try these exercises. Transpose this melody up an octave, keeping it in the bass clef:

Transpose this melody down an octave, putting it into the tenor clef:

Answers

Answers to all these exercises can be found at **www.hybrid publications.com**

Finally, transpose this melody up two octaves, putting it into the treble clef:

Non-octave transpositions

So, octave transpositions are pretty straightforward – it's easy to see if you've made a mistake, and because the transposed version ends up in the same key, you don't need to worry about the key signature. However, if you're transposing by any other interval, the destination key of the transposed material will be different to the key that you have started in. So, the first job when transposing is to transpose the key signature. Take the example below – listen to **Audio track 11** to hear what it sounds like.

Audio track 11

Let's suppose that we want to transpose this excerpt up by a tone. Firstly, work out what the key signature is – in this case, we have a key signature of one sharp, so a reasonable guess would be G major or its relative minor, E minor. For our purposes, it doesn't actually matter whether the key of the excerpt is major or minor, because, once transposed, the new key signature will also work for the new key, whether major or minor.

So, let's assume that the current key signature denotes G major. We're transposing the excerpt up a tone, so we need to transpose the key signature up a tone as well, to A major. So, the new key signature should have three sharps:

Having established the correct key signature we can now proceed to transpose each individual note up by a tone. Providing that we have got the right key signature, if there are no accidentals in the original

Cheating again?

Guitar players use a nifty little device called a *capo* to transpose their entire instrument. It's a small 'clamp' that fits on the neck of the instrument. Placed at the first fret it transposes the instrument up by a semitone, at the second fret by a tone, and so on.

excerpt, we won't require any accidentals in the transposed version:

Listen to **Audio track 12** to hear what this sounds like, and compare back to **track 11**. Can you hear the difference?

Audio track 12

Let's try another one, and this time let's transpose up by the wider interval of a perfect fourth. Here's the original excerpt:

Listen to **Audio track 13** to hear what this sounds like. A key signature of one flat means a key of either F major, or its relative minor, D minor. For the time being, let's assume that the excerpt is in F major. Moving up by a perfect fourth from F major takes us up to B flat major, a key signature of two flats:

Audio track 13

Now it's just a matter of taking each note and transposing up a perfect fourth. Take care when you come to the C♯ notes, though. If you have an accidental in the un-transposed original, you are also going to need an accidental in the transposed version. In this case, transposing up a perfect fourth from C♯ gives us F♯, which isn't included in our new key signature and therefore requires the use of an accidental. At this stage you might think more carefully about why that C♯ appeared in the original excerpt at all. It's certainly a strange note to find in the key of F major, but what about D minor?

Warning sign

If you find yourself adding accidentals in the transposed version that weren't in the original, it's a warning sign that you may have gone wrong.

In D minor, a C♯ would represent the sharpened seventh of the harmonic minor scale, and therefore would be something you would expect to find. This should lead us to suspect that the original key was in fact D minor, and that the transposed key will be G minor, not B flat major as we originally guessed. Our rogue F♯ can now be recognised as the sharpened seventh of the G harmonic minor scale!

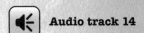 **Audio track 14**

Listen to **Audio track 14** to hear what the transposed version sounds like. Now try these exercises – in each case the stave is left blank for you to insert the appropriate key signature. In this first one, transpose down a minor third:

 Answers

Answers to these exercises can be found at **www.hybrid publications.com**

Here, transpose up a perfect fifth:

Occasionally, you may be asked to transpose something into a different key and a different clef. This is best done in two stages:
1. Make the transposition
2. Rewrite the transposed version in the new clef

So for example, if we were to transpose this melody up a fourth and into the alto clef:

We would first make the transposition:

And then transfer to the alto clef:

Modern score-writing programs like Sibelius and Finale can transpose at the press of a button, but it's still worthwhile perfecting the skill of transposing by hand (and by eye!) as you never know when you will need quickly to transpose a part at a gig, concert or rehearsal. Ultimately, the best way to develop the skill is repeated practice, so start by visiting **www.hybridpublications.com** to find more exercises.

One of the reasons that transposing is such a vital skill for musicians is that there are some instruments that produce higher or lower notes than those that are written. For example, if a clarinet player plays a written A, what we actually hear is the note G. Confused yet? Have no fear, as we are about to explain the world of *transposing instruments...*

Top tip

When faced with the double task of transposing and then writing in a different clef, it's always best to do the transposition in the clef that you're most familiar with. So, if you're asked to move a passage from the alto clef to the treble clef, change the clef first and then do the transposition. If you're moving from the treble clef to the alto, then do the transposition first and then the clef change.

Online material

Visit **www.hybrid publications.com** for more transposition tests.

Transposing instruments

A *transposing instrument* is simply an instrument where the pitch produced is different to that notated. So, in the example given on the previous page, if a clarinettist sees the note A written down and plays it, the note that is actually produced is a G. An even simpler example is the double bass, which is notated an octave higher than it sounds. This is simply because the notes produced by the double bass are too low to be conveniently notated on the bass clef, so the convention is adopted that all double bass music is notated an octave higher.

One might quite legitimately wonder why on earth musicians should invent something as potentially confusing as transposing instruments. As it happens, there are many reasons for their evolution, the most convincing being that they were originally part of a larger family of instruments in different sizes. For example, there were originally several different sizes of clarinet, covering different ranges; the larger ones covering lower ranges than the smaller ones. From the point of view of a clarinettist, it was more convenient for all the different clarinets to have the same fingering, so that he or she could pick up any instrument from the family with equal ease.

In order to allow identical fingering across instruments of different ranges, the simplest solution was to write notes that were fingered the same way as the same pitch. In other words, the different sizes of clarinet all transposed by different amounts. This makes life easy for the clarinettist, who only has to remember one set of fingerings, but makes life harder for composers and arrangers, who have to remember to transpose their parts for the appropriate clarinet.

Gradually, over time, most of the other sizes of clarinet have fallen from use, and we are just left with one size, which happens to be the one that produces notes a tone below those that are notated. Non-transposing instruments are said to be 'in C', because when you notate a C for a non-transposing instrument, what you hear is C. The clarinet is therefore called the Clarinet in B♭, because when it plays a notated C, we hear a B♭.

Handy hint

Transposing instruments are confined to the woodwind and brass families of instruments. Stringed instruments are all in C.

Here's a quick summary of the main transposing instruments:

Clarinet	in B♭
Trumpet	in B♭
Tenor Saxophone	in B♭
Horn	in F
Alto Saxophone	in E♭

There are many others, but these are the ones that you are most likely to come across.

So, to summarise, the clarinet, trumpet and tenor saxophone are instruments in B♭ – that is to say that when they play a notated C, we hear a tone below (B♭). Similarly, when a horn player plays a C, we hear the fifth below (F), and when an alto saxophonist plays a C, we hear a major sixth below (E♭).

The slightly confusing upshot of this is that if we want to get a C note out a a clarinet we need to write a D (that is, the note a tone *above* the one we want). So, if what we want to hear is:

What we need to write is:

The whole sequence has been transposed up a tone, so that, when played back on the clarinet, it will sound a tone lower, giving us the notes that we originally started with. Still confused? Don't worry, this is one area of music theory that many people find difficult. Re-read these two pages until they start to make sense!

Give it a go

If you have friends that play woodwind or brass instruments why not try transposing some music for them. They'll soon let you know if you've made any mistakes...

Jargon buster

Concert pitch is a phrase that musicians use to mean the pitch of notes that we actually hear, as opposed to the written pitch, which, for a transposing instrument, will be different.

Let's imagine a real life situation in which you might need to use transposing instruments. Imagine that you have written a piece of music that requires a brass section containing trumpets and alto saxophones. You book a recording session and need to prepare parts for the players at the session. Here's the part that you want them to play, notated at *concert pitch*:

Remember, concert pitch means the pitch that we are going to hear when the music is played. If you give these parts to the trumpet and sax players, you'll hear something very different, so you need to transpose their parts for the session.

The trumpet is in B♭. So, when the trumpet player plays a notated C, we will hear a B♭, which means that we need to transpose his or her part *up* a tone to get the desired effect:

However, the alto sax is in E♭. So when the saxophonist plays a notated C, we hear the E♭ a major sixth below, and in order to get the notes that we want, we therefore have to transpose the part up a major sixth, like this:

Transposition exercises

Let's practise a few transposition exercises. In the first exercise, you're given a series of notes, played on different instruments. For each instrument, the first note represents the notated pitch – in each case, write the actual sounding pitch next to it.

Hint: not all of these are transposing instruments! This next passage is written for a C instrument. Write it out again below for an instrument in B♭:

Answers

Answers to all these exercises can be found at **www.hybrid publications.com**

Now here's a melody for trumpet in B♭. Write it out again below for Alto Saxophone in E♭ (you might find it easier to do this in two stages). To give you a hand, we've added the correct key signature for you:

Now let's do a couple of exercises where we start with a transposed part and we convert it back into concert pitch. In the first exercise, you're given a series of notes, played on different instruments. For each instrument, the first note represents the sounding pitch – in each case, add the written pitch that would result in this sounding note next to it. Again, beware, not all of these are transposing instruments!

Clarinet   Oboe   Trumpet   Horn

Here's a part for trumpet in B♭. Transpose it back into concert pitch, remember to add the correct key signature:

Now here's a part for alto saxophone in E♭. Again, write out a version in concert pitch:

Lesser-known transposing instruments

The list of transposing instruments on page 71 covers the most commonly-found examples. However, there are a couple of other notable transposing instruments that are worth mentioning:

- The piccolo sounds an octave higher than written.
- The soprano saxophone and the cornet are in B♭.
- As well as the B♭ clarinet, there are also lesser-used clarinets in A and G, and an alto clarinet in E♭, as well as a bass clarinet in B♭ that sounds an octave below the standard clarinet in B♭.
- As well as the B♭ trumpet, there are also trumpets in A and D.
- All guitars sound an octave lower than written.

Try these exercises to practise some of the less common transpositions. Here's a part for clarinet in A – write it out again at concert pitch:

Brassed off

All the instruments in brass bands are transposing instruments in either B♭ or E♭ and are written in the treble clef (with the exception of the bass trombone).

Answers

Answers to all these exercises can be found at **www.hybrid publications.com**

For each instrument listed below, write the note that would have to be written in order for the instrument to produce the note middle C:

Trumpet in D　　*Guitar*　　*Cornet*　　*Clarinet in A*

Worksheet 5 (answers on page 163)

1. Transpose this melody down an octave, putting it into the tenor clef:

2. Transpose this melody up a major third:

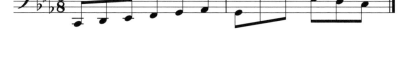

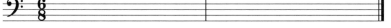

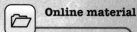
3. Transpose this melody up a perfect fifth and into the treble clef:

4. For each instrument, the given note represents the sounding pitch – in each case, add the written pitch that would result in this sounding note next to it.

Clarinet   Oboe   Trumpet   Horn

Chapter 6:
Time Signatures

In this chapter we will complete your knowledge of time signatures. But first, let's recap briefly on the basics.

A time signature appears at the beginning of a piece of music, along with the key signature. However, unlike the key signature, it is not repeated on every subsequent stave; unless there is a change in time signature later in the piece you will only find it at the beginning. The time signature defines what we call the *meter* of a piece of music – that is to say, the number of beats in each bar, the type of beat, and how those beats are subdivided.

The most common form of time signatures are described as *simple* – this just means that each beat of the bar can be divided into two. So, for example, 4/4 falls into this category because each crotchet beat can be divided into two to form quaver subdivisions.

Listen to **Audio track 15** to hear this example in 4/4. Try counting along, from one to four; once you've got this going, you should be able to put an 'and' in between each number as you count: 'one and two and three and four and'. No matter how many beats in the bar, if you can do this, then the time signature is *simple*.

Examples of simple time signatures include 2/4, 3/4 and 4/4 (crotchet beats), 2/2, 3/2 and 4/2 (minim beats) and 3/8 (quaver beats).

Common time

Remember that 4/4 can be notated instead as a large 'C', which stands for 'common time'. Similarly, 2/2 can be notated as a 'C' with a line through it, which stands for 'cut common' time.

Audio track 15

Online material

Visit **www.hybrid publications.com** to revise simple time signatures.

Online material

Visit **www.hybrid publications.com** to revise compound time signatures.

The other type of time signature you are likely to come across is the *compound* time signature, in which each beat is subdivided into three, rather than two. 6/8 is an example of a compound time signature – the top number tells us to expect six beats per bar and the bottom number tells us that they will be quavers. However, we've already come across a time signature that has six quavers per bar, and that's 3/4:

Audio track 16

Listen to **Audio track 16** to hear what this sounds like. Note that because 3/4 is a *simple* time signature, each of the three crotchet beats is divided into two quavers, giving us a total of six quavers per bar. Now compare this with the same notes, but in 6/8:

Audio track 17

Math rock

A sub-genre of rock music has developed over recent years that is characterised by rapidly changing time signatures and is known as 'math-rock'.

Listen to **Audio track 17** to hear what this sounds like and compare back to **Audio track 16**. Can you hear the difference?

You should be able to hear, and indeed, see, that in 6/8 the quavers are arranged in two groups of three, whereas in 3/4 they are arranged in three groups of two. In effect, in 6/8 there are two 'main' beats of the bar, each worth a dotted crotchet – these 'main' beats are then subdivided into 'sub-beats' of three quavers each. It is this dual nature that explains why meters like 6/8 are labelled as *compound* time signatures. Other examples of compound time signatures include 9/8 and 12/8 (dotted crotchet beats) and 6/16, 9/16 and 12/16 (dotted quaver beats).

Grouping notes in compound time

The use of ties and beams in compound time is slightly more complicated than in simple time. This is just because the system of rhythmic notation is very good at representing note values in divisions of two (we can easily double or halve note values); it is not set up to represent divisions of three quite so well.

One fundamental rule that applies to all time signatures is that notes should be grouped together in beats. This is purely for practical reasons – musicians need to be able to see, at a glance, which notes belong to which beat, and we can help them to do this by clearly grouping them together (using beams and ties) to show where beats begin and end.

So, as we've seen, in 6/8, quavers should always be beamed together in groups of three, like this:

The eye can now quickly see which quavers belong to the first beat and which to the second. Any other beaming pattern would be confusing and counter-intuitive. These groupings are maintained even when we introduce shorter note values, like semiquavers:

Ties and slurs

Ties and slurs look very similar but have very different functions. Slurs can only be used over notes of different pitch and indicate that they should be played *legato*. Ties can only be used between notes of the same pitch as they represent one single note that lasts for the length of all the tied notes added together.

This principle of grouping notes together into beats also applies when using ties. Where a note sounds across the beat, we should notate the rhythm in such a way that we can still see clearly where the beat division occurs: So, for example we wouldn't write this:

When we could write this:

Another universal principle is that we should always try to use the simplest note values possible to represent any given notation. So for example, in a compound time signature like 12/8, if we wanted to represent a note that lasted for two beats, we wouldn't write:

When we could write:

By removing the tied notes we simplify the notation, making it easier to read. Similarly, if we want to represent a note that lasted for three beats we would write it like this:

Not like these two examples:

Note that in the example above we prefer the example where the dotted minim is tied to the dotted crotchet, rather than *vice versa*. This is because we want to try to maintain symmetry around the middle of the bar. In every meter, the first beat of the bar is the strongest, but in meters with four beats in the bar, there is also a strong feeling that the middle (third) beat of the bar has a subsidiary accent. We try to reflect this subdivision by avoiding note values that cross the halfway point of the bar.

Rests in compound time

Like notes, rests in compound time are a little more complicated. Fear not though, there are just a few simple points to be aware of. Firstly, a reminder that in all time signatures (apart from 4/2 – more on that later) a full bar's rest is indicated by a semibreve rest, whether or not the number of beats in the bar adds up to four. This therefore applies to all compound time signatures:

Mind the dot 🔅

When two dotted notes are tied together, be careful where you draw the end of the tie, and make sure that it doesn't obscure or interfere with the dot. Otherwise the rhythm could be misread.

Online material 📂

Visit **www.hybrid publications.com** to find out more about beaming.

Secondly, where we can simplify multiple rests into longer rest values (*within* one beat) we should always do so. This keeps the music tidy and reduces the number of symbols on the page that a musician needs to read and interpret. So, for example, rather than using three quaver rests, one after another, replace them with a single dotted crotchet rest:

Style file

Not all aspects of music theory are set in stone. Some elements of style vary from place to place. The use of dotted rests is frowned on by some publishers, while others encourage the practice.

Note that a crotchet rest followed by a quaver rest would have the same effect, and isn't wrong; however, the dotted crotchet rest is tidier and leaves more space on the stave and is therefore generally preferred. If using this style of notation, the crotchet rest should always come before the quaver rest, and never after.

Just like notes, rests in compound time should always be grouped according to the beats of the bar. So for example, a rest lasting four quavers in 6/8 should be represented like this:

So that we can clearly see the beat divisions, and not like this:

Where the beat division is obscured by the fact that the second crotchet rest crosses the divide between between beat one and beat two.

Counting in minims

Let's continue this chapter with a look at some of the less common time signatures that you may encounter, starting with 2/2. A look at the top and bottom numbers of this time signature will quickly reveal that we should expect two minim beats per bar:

Listen to **Audio track 18** to hear what this sounds like. Some of you may have spotted this that meter is very similar to 4/4 (or *common time*) – both allow for four crotchets per bar, after all, so why bother having two different time signatures? However, there is a subtle difference between 2/2 and 4/4. 2/2 is a *duple* time signature – that is to say that it defines two beats per bar, whereas 4/4 defines four beats per bar. In practice, the difference between the two usually comes down to the *feel* of the meter; some pieces are obviously in four, while others fall more naturally into two. The boundary between the two is further blurred by the fact that, as we have seen, quadruple meters like 4/4 have a subsidiary accent on the third beat of the bar, which can, depending on the tempo, encourage the feeling of a minim pulse rather than a crotchet one. The connection between the two meters is underlined by their alternative names: 4/4 is also known as *common time*, while 2/2 is known as *cut common time*.

Audio track 18

The C symbol is therefore sometimes used as an alternative for 4/4, while the C with a line through it is substituted for 2/2.

3/2 and 4/2 time signatures are also used, although they are less commonly found. 3/2 has the same relation to 6/4 as 2/2 has to 4/4: 6/4 has six crotchet beats per bar, whereas 3/2 has three minim beats.

4/2 has four minim beats per bar and is notable mainly for the fact that it is the only time signature in which a whole bar's rest is not indicated by a semibreve rest, but rather by a breve rest:

Answers

Answers to these exercises can be found at **www.hybrid publications.com**

In this exercise, the top exercise is in 4/4. Write it out again below in 4/2, doubling each note value:

Look out for that whole bar's rest!

Counting in semiquavers

Time signatures like 2/4, 3/4 and 4/4, and 6/8, 9/8 and 12/8 are by far the most commonly found. However, as we have seen, time signatures with a minim pulse are also used; similarly time signatures with a semiquaver pulse are also employed from time to time.

In theory, both simple and compound time signatures with a semiquaver pulse are possible: 2/16, 3/16 and 4/16 are examples of simple meters with a semiquaver pulse, while 6/16, 9/16 and 12/6 are examples of compound meters. In practice, 2/16 and 4/16 are very rare, with 2/4 and 4/4 being preferred, with the relevant change in tempo being applied to achieve the desired rhythmic effect.

However, the compound meters are used so it is worthwhile familiarising yourself with them. The same rules about beaming in groups and the use of ties apply in these time signatures, as they do in 6/8, 9/8 and 12/8: notes should always be beamed in beats and ties should be used to ensure that beat divisions are clearly visible:

As do the rules relating to the use of rests:

All of the time signatures that you've encountered so far have involved regularly repeating groups of two, three or four beats per bar. For this reason, they are known as *regular* time signatures. To finish this chapter we are now going to take a look at a special group of time signatures that do not follow this pattern – the *irregular* time signatures.

Top tip

Time signatures with a minim or semiquaver pulse are rarer because they are at the outer edge of the note value spectrum. For example, in the interests of readability, composers will often prefer to double the b.p.m. marking of a piece and write it out in quavers, rather than fill the page with semiquavers, which can look very 'black' and intimidating.

Irregular time signatures

Back in 'How To Read Music', when we introduced the concept of time signatures, we said that the upper note of a time signature, could, in theory, represent any number of beats per bar. However, since then we've tended to concentrate on meters with two, three or four beats per bar. Compound time signatures, which subdivide these main beats of the bar into threes, give us top numbers of six, nine and 12.

We don't tend to see numbers greater than 12 at the top of time signatures (except in some modern scores) because the human mind breaks down larger groups of beats into smaller, more easily understandable, subgroupings of two, three or four.

All of these time signatures have one thing in common – they are divisible by two or three. In other words, every time signature that we've looked at so far can be simplified into a meter that essentially has two or three beats per bar.

It is possible to imagine some time signatures that would not abide by this rule; for example, any time signature with a prime number at the top of it cannot (by definition) be broken down into smaller subdivisions. (Readers of a mathematical bent will no doubt point out that two and three are also prime numbers, but should note that these also cannot be broken down any further!) These meters are known as *irregular* time signatures.

While the above mathematical definition has the virtue of a certain elegance, in practice, musicians call any time signature that is not duple, triple or quadruple an irregular time signature. The two most commonly used upper figures are five and seven, giving us time signatures of 5/4, 7/4, 5/8, 7/8 etc.

While these meters cannot be simplified into regular patterns of twos or threes, they can be understood as combinations of two- and three-note groupings. So, for example, 5/4 can be thought of as a grouping of three crotchets followed by a grouping of two crotchets:

Irrational?

Some modern scores also use *irrational* time signatures, where the bottom number of the time signature is not divisible by 2. For example, 4/5, is an irrational time signature that indicates a bar with five beats, each of which is worth a fifth of a semibreve or whole note.

Listen to **Audio track 19** to hear what this sounds like.

Audio track 19

Similarly, 5/8 can be thought of as a group of three quavers followed by a group of two quavers:

In five

Famous tunes in 5/4 include:
Take Five
Dave Brubeck
Good Morning
The Beatles
Seven Days
Sting
Living In The Past
Jethro Tull

When first encountered, a meter with five beats per bar can seem unnatural and difficult, but by thinking of it as a group of three beats followed by a group of two, it suddenly becomes more intelligible. Indeed, pieces 'in five' are more common than you might think – check out some of the tunes in the sidebar and try counting along.

In a similar way, the time signatures of 7/4 and 7/8 can be understood as a grouping of three beats followed by a grouping of four beats (or *vice versa*):

The 3+4 and 4+3 groupings can be used interchangeably, depending on the composer's wishes.

Beams and ties in irregular time signatures

Once the subdivisions of the irregular time signature have been understood then the basic rules of beaming and note groupings still apply. All beams and ties should be used in such a way that the underlying groupings of two and three are clearly visible. So, for example, in this first first example in 5/4, the beams and ties allow the underlying 3+2 pattern to be seen clearly:

However, if the underlying grouping was 2+3 (which is less common) then we could write exactly the same note values like this, which makes the 2+3 structure explicit:

The same principle applies for the use of rests – they should never cut across the underlying subdivisions of five or seven. So, for example, this would be incorrect:

While this maintains the 4+3 quaver subdivisions:

Let's finish this chapter with some exercises to test your knowledge of irregular time signatures. Start by beaming these bars of 7/8 correctly to reflect a 3+4 subdivision:

Now fill in the rests in this example in 5/4 (3+2):

Finally, can you deduce the correct subdivision of this example of 7/4 just by looking at the note values used and the way in which the notes have been beamed?

Answers

Answers to all these exercises can be found at **www.hybrid publications.com**

Worksheet 6 (answers on page 164)

1. Add beams to this example in 9/8:

2. Add beams to this example in 5/8 to show a subdivision of 3+2:

3. Write out this melody in 6/16, halving each note value:

4. Which of these is not an irregular time signature?
5/4, 7/8, 9/8, 11/16

Chapter 7:
General Musicianship

At this point we're going to take a breather from the nitty gritty of music theory and think about some of the wider knowledge that musicians need and use on a daily basis. While most of what follows can't be said, therefore, to fall under the heading of 'music theory' it is, nonetheless, a vital part of a musical education.

In particular, we're going to introduce some detailed information about the instruments of the orchestra, the instrumental families that they belong to, and their particular idiosyncrasies – the aim being to provide enough information for you to converse knowledgably with other musicians, or perhaps to pique your interest enough to investigate further.

The instruments of the orchestra

Even if you don't play an orchestral instrument, it's worth spending a little time familiarising yourself with the key facts about each one. At the very least, an understanding of the fundamentals of how an instrument works (and therefore its limitations and specialities) will allow you to appreciate the skill involved in playing it, and to communicate with instrumental players if you ever need to work with them in performance, or in composition and arrangement.

Of course there are many instruments that do not fall into the category of 'orchestral instruments': the voice (which we class as an instrument), keyboard instruments (piano, harpsichord, celeste etc.), many stringed and fretted instruments, as well as those associated with folk music, popular music and other music traditions around the world.

However, the fact remains that the orchestra is a good place to start, and some key bits of knowledge in this area will stand you in good stead for the future.

Get historical

A basic grasp of the history of music and its most important characters is also a vital part of a musical education. Space doesn't permit a discussion here, but we recommend Donald Jay Grout's *History of Western Music* (Norton & Co.).

Organisation of the orchestra

At first glance the orchestra seems like a large group of musicians gathered somewhat randomly around the conductor in the centre. However, the layout of the orchestra reflects the fact that it is made up of 'families' of instruments. Each family is grouped together physically, and sonically, because instruments within the same family share certain characteristics – primarily the way in which they produce sound.

The main instrument families within the orchestra are:

Strings
Woodwind
Brass
Percussion

And this is how they are laid out in the orchestra:

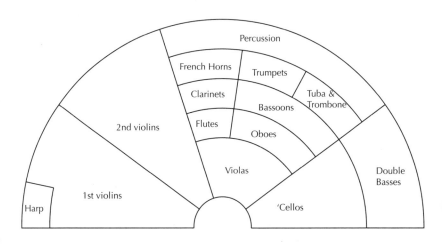

As you can see, the strings form the centre of the orchestra, clustered around the conductor, with brass and woodwind arrayed behind them. The percussion (where present) brings up the rear. Let's take a more detailed look at each instrument family in turn...

The string family

The names of the different instrument families are prosaically descriptive and so it should come as no surprise that the string family (usually known as the *string section*) is a group of instruments in which the sound is produced by vibrating strings. In particular, the string section is a family of instruments in which sound is generated by strings that are caused to vibrate by dragging a *bow* across them.

The bow is essentially a long narrow wooden pole – between the two ends of the pole are stretched several hundred horse hairs. The bow holds the hairs securely in place and keeps them taut via a tightening mechanism. String players rub rosin (a sticky substance derived from resin) onto the bow each time that they play, in order to get the hair to 'grip' the string and produce the desired vibration.

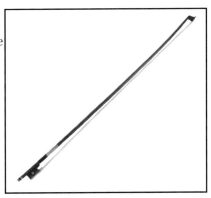

The vibration of the strings is transferred to the rest of the instrument via the bridge, where the hollow body amplifies the vibration, allowing it to be heard. The pitch of the vibrating string is determined by its length, thickness and tension. Short, thin strings produce higher notes while longer, fatter strings produce lower ones. For this reason, the smaller stringed instruments have higher ranges, while the larger ones have lower ones.

The most common members of the string family are the violin, the viola, the 'cello and the double bass.

The Strad

The most famous violin maker is undoubtedly Antonio Stradivarius. Born in Italy in 1644, he actually made violins, violas and 'cellos, as well as a small number of guitars, mandolins and harps.

Tuning

The strings on stringed instruments are usually tuned in fifths (with the exception of the double bass). The tuning can be altered, either by twisting the wooden tuning pegs, to make large changes, or by adjusting the fine tuners on the tailpiece, to make small changes in tuning.

String techniques

As described above, the normal method of sound production on a stringed instrument is to drag the bow across the string. The bow can be dragged from the end where it is held – called the *heel* – to the tip (this is called a *down-bow*) or in the opposite direction (called an *up-bow*). When down-bows and up-bows need to be specified in notation the symbols ⊓ and ⋁ are used. In violin notation, it is assumed that the strings will be bowed; if this needs to be made explicit then the indication *arco* is used.

Very occasionally, string players are asked to turn their bow upside down and drag the wooden part of the bow across the strings. This is indicated by the term *col legno* (literally, *with wood*). The other important method of sound production for string players is to discard the bow and pluck the strings with the fingers. This is known as *pizzicato* (and is usually abbreviated to *pizz.*).

Another technique available to string players is to move the bow from its usual position, between the bridge and the fingerboard, to play either directly over the bridge, or over the fingerboard. Both these techniques produce distinctive sounds, and are notated as *sul ponticello* and *sul tasto* respectively. String players can also use the natural springiness of the bow to bounce it off the strings, producing a unique style of playing known as *spiccato*.

Finally, string players have the option of using mutes to alter the sound of their instruments. Mutes are small devices that are fitted to the bridge of the instrument, reducing the amount of string vibration that is transferred via the bridge to the body. Mutes therefore reduce the volume of the instrument, but they also alter the tonal quality, boosting some frequencies while attenuating others.

In string notation the term *con sordini* (abbreviated to *con sord.*) is used to indicate that mutes should be used. *Senza sordini* (*senza sord.*) indicates that mutes should be removed.

The Violin

Clef: Treble
Transposing: No (C)
Tuned: G D A E
Range:

The smallest of the string instruments, the violin has four strings, tuned in fifths. There are more violins in the orchestra than any other instrument and they are typically divided into two subgroups, called the first and second violins. Each section has a leader, and the leader of the first violins is also known as the leader of the orchestra. The first violins typically play the top line of the string texture, and their part tends to be more technically challenging.

The Viola

Clef: Alto and Treble
Transposing: No (C)
Tuned: C G D A
Range:

Essentially a scaled-up violin, the viola is also tuned in fifths, but sounds a fifth lower than the violin. Its timbre is also noticeably different – woodier and more mellow. Due to its lower range, the viola reads mostly from the alto clef; however for higher passages the treble clef can be used. It sits in the centre of the string section, both physically and sonically.

Playing chords

Stringed instruments can play up to two notes at once, since only two strings can be bowed at the same time (this is known as double-stopping). Chords of up to four notes can only be played by 'rocking' the bow across the strings.

Online material

Visit **www.hybrid publications.com** to explore suggested listening for the violin and viola.

The 'Cello

Clef: Bass, Tenor, Treble
Transposing: No (C)
Tuned: C G D A
Range:

The 'cello's full name is the violoncello. Unlike the viola and violin it is not held under the chin, but, due to its bulk, is rested on the floor on a large 'spike' that protrudes from the bottom of the instrument, with the player seated. Although 'cello notation is mostly in the bass clef, the tenor and treble clefs can be used for higher passages.

The Double Bass

Clef: Bass
Transposing: C, 8ve lower
Tuned: E A D G
Range:

The largest member of the string family, the double bass differs from the violin, viola and 'cello in several respects. Firstly, it is tuned in fourths, not fifths – this is at least partly due to its size, which makes stretching for larger intervals more taxing. Secondly, its proportions are different, with the 'shoulders' of the instrument being less pronounced. The bottom string of the double bass can be extended to allow access to even lower pitches, while some double basses have a fifth, lower string, tuned a fifth below the bottom E string. Double basses sound an octave lower than notated.

The bass

The double bass is frequently used in other genres of music, apart from Western Classical music. It plays an important role in jazz, blues, rock'n'roll and bluegrass music.

Online material

Visit **www.hybrid publications.com** to explore suggested listening for the 'cello and double bass.

The woodwind family

Again, the name of the woodwind family gives us a clue as to how they generate sound – in this case the clue is in the 'wind', as sound is generated by the player blowing air through the instrument. However, not all woodwind instruments are made of wood, so don't take the name too literally.

There are two key methods by which woodwind instruments convert blown air into sound: the first is through the use of a *reed*, a thin piece of cane that vibrates when air is blown past it. The second method is to blow air across a thin edge, which splits the flow of air, causing the sound.

The reed method of sound production breaks down into two further subdivisions. Single-reed instruments have one reed that is fitted into a mouthpiece; air is then forced between the reed and the mouthpiece, causing the air to vibrate. Double-reed instruments have (you guessed it) two reeds, which are fitted against each other; air is then forced between them to create the necessary vibration.

Within the woodwind family, clarinets are single-reed instruments, while oboes and bassoons are double-reed instruments. Flutes and piccolos use the 'edge method' of sound generation.

There is one notable member of the woodwind family that is not included in the standard orchestra – the saxophone. This single-reed instrument was invented by Adolphe Sax in the 1840s, by which time the composition of the orchestra had largely been established. The saxophone comes in a variety of sizes and keys and is frequently mistaken for a brass instrument due to the fact that its body is constructed of metal.

All woodwind instruments use a system of keys to open and close holes in the body of the instrument, thus creating the different notes. Flutes are usually made of brass or alloys, while oboes and bassoons can be made of wood, plastic, hard rubber or other composite materials.

The recorder

One very common woodwind instrument that is not part of the orchestra is the recorder. Many people have unpleasant memories of learning the recorder at school and may be surprised to hear that, played properly, it makes a very attractive sound.

The Flute

Clef: Treble
Transposing: (No) C
Range:

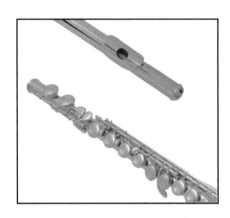

The flute family is a large one, including instruments of many different sizes and in many different keys, but the concert flute normally found in orchestras is as shown above. The piccolo is a smaller member of the flute family, with an even higher range than the flute; it is also in the key of C, but sounds an octave higher than written.

The Clarinet

Clef: Treble
Transposing: B♭
Written range:

Like the flute, the clarinet comes in many different sizes and keys (over 20 different types of clarinet exist), but the most commonly played orchestral clarinet is the version in B♭, as shown above. The clarinet in A is also commonly used in orchestras, with players swapping between instruments in different keys, depending on the demands of the score. The range of the clarinet can be split up into three distinct registers: the bottom third is known as the *chalameau* register (characterised by a rich sound); the middle third is called the *clarinet* register, while the top third is known as the *altissimo* register, and can be rather shrill.

Jazz flute

The flute has been used extensively in jazz by artists such as Eric Dolphy and Herbie Mann. Its most famous proponent in the world of rock was Ian Anderson, of the band Jethro Tull.

Online material

Visit **www.hybrid publications.com** to explore suggested listening for the flute and clarinet.

The Oboe

Clef: Treble
Transposing: (No) C
Range:

The oboe's unique timbre is instantly recognisable. A double-reed instrument, it is generally regarded (along with the French horn) as one of the hardest orchestral instruments to learn to play. It is the oboist's job in the orchestra to provide the tuning note (usually an A at 440 Hz) for the rest of the orchestra to tune to. The *cor anglais* (literally, English horn) is a close relative of the oboe; it sounds a fifth lower than the oboe and is a transposing instrument in F.

The Bassoon

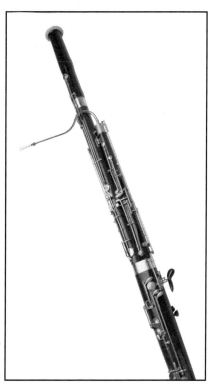

Clef: Bass, tenor, treble
Transposing: (No) C
Range:

Like the oboe, the bassoon is considered a difficult instrument to learn – add to this the fact that the instrument reads from three clefs (bass, tenor and treble) and that bassoons can be extremely expensive and you can see why few people choose to play them! The standard orchestra features two bassoons, sometimes with a contrabassoon, which sounds an octave lower.

Online material

Visit **www.hybrid publications.com** to explore suggested listening for the oboe and bassoon.

The bassoon

In Italian the bassoon is called *Il fagotto*, which literally means 'bundle of firewood'. They are also expensive instruments, so I wouldn't recommend taking the name too literally.

The brass family

Unlike the string and woodwind families, the name of the brass family of instruments is slightly misleading. Although brass instruments do tend to be made of metal, some metal instruments are not part of the brass family, such as the flute and saxophones (and indeed some members of the brass family are made of wood). What all brass instruments do have in common, however, is that sound is produced by the vibration of the lips.

The pitch of the note produced is controlled either by valves, which increase and decrease the length of tubing that the air passes through (as on a trumpet) or by a slide, which achieves the same effect (as on a trombone). In addition, the tension of the player's lips (known as *embouchure*) can alter the pitch of notes produced by causing the column of air to vibrate at different harmonics.

The brass family includes a huge range of instruments, only some of which are included in the standard symphony orchestra. Brass bands, concert bands, marching bands and military bands all feature brass instruments prominently, and instruments, technique and style vary considerably depending on the type of ensemble.

Like the strings, there are various mutes available for brass instruments that change their sound quite dramatically. Typically, mutes are placed inside the bell of the instrument, or clipped onto the outside, and can be made of metal, plastic or cardboard. They come in various different varieties, including straight mutes (which fit directly into the bell), cup mutes (similar to straight mutes but with an additional outer 'cup') and wah-wah mutes (which can be operated by the player's free hand to change the instrument's timbre).

Mutes have the side effect of making the instruments play sharp, so brass players have to compensate for this when employing them.

 Spit'n'polish

Because brass players blow into their instrument directly one potential hazard is a build-up of saliva inside. For this reason, brass instruments have small 'keys' that can be used to drain the offending liquid away.

The Trumpet

Clef: Treble
Transposing: B♭
Written range:

The trumpet in B♭ is the highest of the orchestral brass instruments, and is the most commonly used of a family of instruments of differing sizes and keys. The trumpet features three piston valves that are used to alter the length of the tubing; by combining the natural harmonics of the instrument with these valves it is possible to create a complete chromatic scale.

The French Horn

Clef: Bass, Treble
Transposing: F
Written range:

The French horn has a distinctive 'coiled' shape and uses three rotary valves (in contrast to the piston valves used on trumpets). It is considered the most difficult of the brass instruments to play, due to the very precise *embouchure* required to ensure correct intonation. The hornist uses one hand to operate the valves while the other hand can be inserted into the bell of the instrument to fine tune intonation.

Online material

Visit **www.hybrid publications.com** to explore suggested listening for the trombone and tuba.

The Trombone

Clef:	Bass, Tenor and Alto
Transposing:	C
Range:	

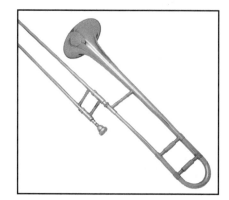

Trombone literally means 'large trumpet' but, unlike the trumpet, which uses valves to alter the length of tubing, the trombone employs a slide which the player can extend. A trombonist uses a combination of *embouchure* and slide to access the full chromatic scale. Because of its unique construction the trombone is able to produce a smooth *glissando,* unlike most other brass instruments.

The Tuba

Clef:	Bass, Tenor
Transposing:	Various
Range:	

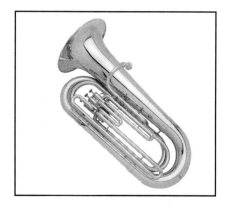

Tuba tubing

Amazingly, the main tube of a B♭ tuba is 18 feet (over five metres) long, and the tube gradually increases in diameter until it reaches the bell.

The tuba is the lowest (and therefore the largest) instrument of the brass family, and uses either rotary valves (like the French horn) or piston valves (like the trumpet). From three to six valves can be used, depending on the manufacturer and key of the instrument. As the bass instrument of the family, the tuba fulfils a similar role to that of the double bass in the string family, and is commonly used in marching bands, brass bands and traditional New Orleans-style jazz bands. The tuba is also increasingly popular as a solo instrument.

The percussion family

The percussion family includes any instruments ranging from the timpani (or kettle drum) though to the glockenspiel or gong. What they all have in common is that they are struck or hit in some way.

Broadly speaking, percussion instruments can be divided into two camps: pitched and unpitched. Pitched percussion instruments include the xylophone and glockenspiel, which are superficially similar, consisting of a collection of bars (wooden and metal, respectively) arranged in the same configuration as a piano keyboard, which are hit with beaters. Other pitched percussion instruments include the marimba, vibraphone and tubular bells.

The timpani are a common site at the back of orchestras, but, unlike most drums, they too fall into the category of tuned percussion. This is because the tension of the drum head is tuned to produce specific notes. There are various systems for controlling this tuning, but most timpani use a system of pedals which allows the pitch to be changed quickly, often during a performance.

Untuned percussion can include instruments like drums (including the drum kit), cymbals and gongs, as well as orchestral whips, guiros, bells, triangles and many others. While most percussionists play every type of percussion instrument, timpanists specialise in the timpani and play nothing else.

Outside of the orchestra, percussion instruments are vital to almost every form of music, from popular music styles like rock, jazz, hip hop and dance music, through to non-western musical traditions and folk music from around the world.

Feeling it

The Scottish percussionist Evelyn Glennie has been deaf since the age of 12, but claims that she has taught herself to 'hear' using other parts of her body, often playing barefoot better to absorb the vibrations.

Online material

Visit **www.hybrid publications.com** to explore suggested listening for drums and percussion.

Instruments from outside the classical tradition

As we mentioned at the start of this chapter, there are many other instruments that are in common use by millions of people around the world that we haven't mentioned yet. In particular, musical cultures all over the globe have developed their own specialist instruments, ranging from the bodhrán in Ireland, to the sitar in India, to the didgeridoo in Australia. Space doesn't permit an in-depth survey of these instruments here, but if you have a particular interest in music from one region then you may find it fascinating to spend some time familiarising yourself with its particular instrumentation.

Popular music, by contrast (and as its name suggests), has become a universal musical style, known around the world. Based around a core line-up of guitar, bass and drums, it has splintered into thousands of subgenres, and relies increasingly on electronic instruments and computers for its effect. Instruments from the classical tradition, such as strings and brass, are often added into arrangements – in fact, pretty much anything goes, with everything from bagpipes to brass bands being used to 'spice up' a pop song. Here we'll restrict ourselves to looking at the key instruments involved in a rock or pop band: the guitar, bass guitar, keyboard and drums.

The Guitar

Clef: Treble
Transposing: C (8ve lower)
Tuned: E A D G B E
Written range:

Guitars can be divided into two main sub-groups: electric guitars and acoustic guitars, which have certain characteristics in common. All tend to have six strings, stretched over a fingerboard across which are

Birth of the axe

Early electric guitars started to appear in the 1930s and 40s, from pioneers like Rickenbacker and Les Paul. The first commercially successful solid-bodied electric guitar was the 1951 Fender Broadcaster, later renamed the Telecaster.

Online material

Visit **www.hybrid publications.com** to explore suggested listening for the guitar.

placed metal markers that indicate where notes are to be found (called frets). The strings are attached at one end to the bridge and at the other end to tuning pegs, mounted on a headstock. One hand is used to hold down the strings, while the other hand picks the string (either with the fingers or with a small plastic device called a *plectrum*), causing it to vibrate. The difference between acoustic and electric guitars is in the way that the sound created by these vibrating strings is amplified.

An acoustic guitar is similar to the violin or viola in that the vibration of the strings is transferred to the hollow body of the instrument by the bridge, which resonates, thus amplifying the sound. Electric guitars, by contrast, tend to have solid wooden bodies. Vibration of the metal strings is converted into an electronic signal by devices called 'pick-ups', and is then fed from the guitar, via a cable, into an amplifier which converts the electronic signal into sound. The advantage of this system is not only that this enables the guitar to be played extremely loudly (and therefore allows it to compete with the sound of drums, brass section etc.), but also that this electronic signal can be manipulated and altered to obtain a huge range of different sounds and effects.

The six strings of the guitar tend to be tuned as shown opposite (this is known as standard tuning). However, the tuning of individual strings (and indeed the number of strings themselves) is often varied to create different harmonic effects. In addition, a clamping device known as a *capo* can be fixed over the fretboard to, in effect, transpose the instrument into different keys. This is frequently used when accompanying singers whose range may demand that a song is transposed.

There are hundreds of different types of acoustic and electric guitars, ranging from 'classical' nylon-strung guitars through to triple-necked electrics; their enduring popularity is testament to their flexibility and adaptability as instruments for creating popular music. Add to this the fact that they can be used for both harmony and melody, and that they are light and easily transportable, and you can see why sales of guitars outstrip those of almost every other instrument.

Key guitarists

Any list of the most influential electric guitarists would have to include:
Jimi Hendrix
Eric Clapton
Mark Knopfler
(Dire Straits)
Jimmy Page
(Led Zeppelin)
Eddie Van Halen
Brian May
(Queen)
Angus Young
(AC/DC)
David Gilmour
(Pink Floyd)
Steve Vai
Carlos Santana
Ritchie Blackmore
(Deep Purple)
Tony Iommi
(Black Sabbath)
... and the list goes on!

The Bass Guitar

Clef: Bass
Transposing: C (8ve lower)
Tuned: E A D G
Range:

Key bassists

Some of the most famous exponents of the electric bass guitar include:
Flea (Red Hot Chili Peppers)
James Jamerson
Jaco Pastorius
Paul McCartney
Stanley Clarke
Mark King (Level 42)
Bootsy Collins
John Paul Jones (Led Zeppelin)

Online material

Visit **www.hybrid publications.com** to explore suggested listening for the bass guitar.

Superficially, the bass guitar looks very similar to the electric guitar, with the main difference being that it has only four strings to the electric guitar's six (although some models can have five or six strings). These four strings are tuned to the same notes as the bottom four strings of the guitar, but an octave lower (the same as the double bass).

The principles of sound production are exactly the same as for the electric guitar, with the vibration of the strings converted by the pick-ups into an electrical signal and fed to an amplifier. The strings themselves are substantially thicker than those found on an electric guitar, since they produce much lower pitches.

Like the electric guitar, the bass guitar can be picked or played with the fingers, although the latter is far more common amongst bassists than it is amongst guitarists. Some additional techniques are also available, including slapping or 'popping' the strings with the picking hand. While most bass guitars do have frets, fretless versions are available, and have a distinctive sound, allowing true *glissandos* and other expressive effects.

Guitar notation

While the electric guitar and bass guitar can read from the treble and bass clefs respectively, many players prefer to read from a system called *tablature*. Rather than displaying the notes to be played, tablature (or tab, for short) instead indicates where you should place your fingers on the instrument, and has been used for fretted instruments since the Renaissance at least, and possibly earlier.

A guitar tab stave looks like this:

The six lines running horizontally represent the six strings of the guitar (a bass tab stave would only have four lines, therefore). The bottom line represents the lowest string (the bottom E string), the next line up represents the A string, and so on, up to the high E string, which is represented by the top line. Numbers are placed on these lines to indicate where notes should be fretted. So for example, a '3' appearing on the bottom line indicates that a note should be fretted at the third fret on the bottom string, while a '0' indicates that no note should be fretted and that the string should be played 'open'. Notes written vertically above one another are to be played at the same time; for example, the tab below shows a C major chord:

Other indications like phrasing, articulation and special guitar techniques can also be included in the tablature, some of which cannot be represented in traditional music notation. Most tablature does not include rests or rhythmic notation, and for that reason it is often presented alongside traditional notation, which can represent rhythmic information very clearly. The combination of the two types of notation gives the guitarist all the information required to perform the piece of music accurately. The example overleaf shows how the two types of notation work together:

Chord symbols

Other types of notation used by guitarists include chord symbols, which specify the harmony to be used (e.g. E7, Asus4) while leaving the exact voicing and finger positions up to the guitarist and chord boxes, which specify exactly where each finger should be placed on the fretboard.

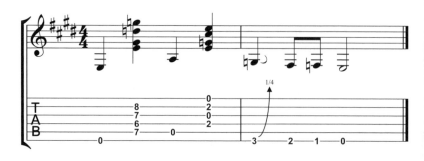

Drums

Clef:	Percussion
Transposing:	N/A
Tuned:	N/A
Range:	N/A

The drum kit is a familiar sight at the back of most rock and pop groups and consists of a collection of different drums, cymbals and other untuned percussion. At the bare minimum it is likely to consist of a bass drum (played with a foot pedal), a snare drum, several 'toms', a hi-hat cymbal (also operated by a foot pedal although it can also be played with sticks), a ride cymbal and a crash cymbal.

Each drum and cymbal has a slightly different timbre and effect. The number of additional drums is down to the individual player, and can be further augmented with other instruments such as cow-bell or tambourine.

Drums and cymbals are usually played with wooden drumsticks, apart from the bass drum and hi-hat cymbal, which are operated from foot pedals, but occasionally softer 'brushes' can be used for a different effect.

Drums are notated on a five-line stave, with different positions on the stave representing the different drums and cymbals. Since the drum kit consists almost entirely of unpitched instruments, none of the traditional clefs is appropriate, and a 'neutral' clef consisting of two short vertical lines is used, as shown below:

Keyboard

Clef:	Treble and bass
Transposing:	C
Tuned:	N/A
Range:	Varies

In many pop and rock groups the basic trio format of guitar, bass and drums is augmented with an electronic keyboard, which may or may not be allied to other bits of technology including computers, sequencers and effects units. The electronic keyboard started to come to prominence in the 1970s, as musicians embraced emerging technology to create new sounds. Early models were large and cumbersome, but they soon shrank; by the 1980s models like the Roland DX-7 became hugely popular and influenced a generation of musicians. These days, a keyboard is basically a simple piano-style interface which allows a musician to call up a host of sampled sounds from a computer and manipulate them.

In practical terms this has huge advantages as one bit of equipment can stand in for a piano, harpsichord or organ, or even a string or brass section. For many amateur musicians, keyboards offer an affordable way to access sounds and instruments that they would otherwise be unable to use.

Key keys

And on the keys, check out some of these guys:
Keith Emerson
Rick Wakeman
(Yes)
Ray Manzarek
(The Doors)
Jean Michel Jarre
Stevie Wonder
Elton John

Online material

Visit **www.hybrid publications.com** to explore suggested listening for the electronic keyboard.

Worksheet 7 (answers on page 165)

1. How many strings do instruments in the string family of instruments have?

2. What is the lowest member of the string family?

3. Join up these Italian string techniques with their correct English counterparts:

col legno	play over the bridge
pizzicato	play over the fingerboard
sul tasto	pluck the strings
sul ponticello	use the wood of the bow

4. Which of these is a double reed instrument?

A. Trumpet

B. Oboe

C. Viola

D. Flute

5. Join each instrument up with its correct key:

Flute	B flat
Trumpet	F
Alto Saxophone	C
French Horn	E flat

6. How many strings does a guitar have?

Answers

Answers to this worksheet can be found on page 165.

Online material

Additional worksheets are available at **www.hybrid publications.com**.

Chapter 8:
Composition (Part 1)

Composition simply means the creation of music. This might be music that is created on the spur of the moment, as in improvisation, or it might be written down by a composer and then passed to a group of musicians to play. These days it is even more likely to be created and reproduced on a computer.

Music theory is a tool that can help us, not only to understand and play compositions written by other people, but to compose music ourselves, in whichever style interests us, whether it's big band, string quartets or dance music. In this chapter we'll explore some simple rules that will allow you to use your knowledge of music theory to start to compose.

Many people find the thought of creating their own music daunting because they don't know where to start, rather like trying to write a novel by sitting down with a blank piece of paper in front of you. However, because music is based around ideas of repetition, development and embellishment, you will find that once you start to apply some simple principles you will find it easier than you thought possible.

Questions and answers

Let's keep things really simple to start with and just consider rhythm. Below, you'll see a rhythmic phrase, which you can also hear on **Audio track 20**.

Define me!

The guitarist and composer Frank Zappa once defined a composer as "a guy who goes around forcing his will on unsuspecting air molecules, often with the assistance of unsuspecting musicians".

Audio track 20

Try to imagine a second phrase that would sound good after this one. Try clapping it rhythmically a couple of times and then see if you can write the rhythmic notation in the space provided above.

Call & Response

The idea of "call and response" can be found in many different types of music, from the antiphonal effects of 16th-century composer Gabrieli, through to the traditional work songs of African-American slaves.

Audio track 21

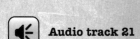

Audio track 22

It might help to imagine that the first phrase is a question and that you are supplying the answer – this 'call and response' pattern is very common in music.

It's important to remember that there is no such thing as a 'right' or 'wrong' answer to this exercise. The only thing that you should be aiming for is to create something that sounds musically satisfying to you. For example, one possible answering phrase could look like this:

Listen to **Audio track 21** to hear what this sounds like. Notice how the answering phrase takes the rhythm of the opening phrase and repeats it almost exactly, with a slight change at the end. Contrary to what you might think, repetition in music is a desirable quality – our ears (and brains) find repeated patterns attractive, so when attempting an exercise like this, it's always a good idea to find some element of the opening phrase that you can repeat.

Here's another rhythm, in a different time signature – listen to **Audio track 22** to hear what it sounds like, and then see if you can come up with an answering rhythm:

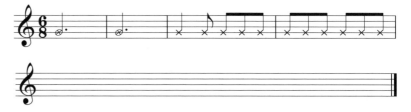

Again, here's a sample answering phrase that we've come up with:

As before, remember that this is only one of many possible, and equally musically satisfying endings. In this case, we've used another handy musical technique and have reversed the pattern of the opening phrase, which starts with long note values and moves to shorter ones, to give an answering phrase that starts with shorter note values and moves on to longer ones. Again, this is something that we, as listeners, find satisfying. Listen to **Audio track 23** to hear what it sounds like.

Audio track 23

Here's another opening rhythm for you to try; listen to **Audio track 24** to hear what it sounds like. This time try using the technique described above and reverse the pattern of note values:

Audio track 24

Another approach is to create an answering phrase that contrasts with the opening phrase. So, for example, if the opening phrase moves slowly, create an answering rhythm that moves more rapidly, or *vice versa*. Here are a couple more opening rhythms for you to practise with:

Backwards?

Reversing something in music is often given the name "retrograde" (literally, "backwards"). Rhythms and melodies can often be reversed to create new material.

In each case, try to identify something unique about the opening pattern, and use that as inspiration for your answering phrase, but above all, be guided by your own musical instinct.

So, to summarise, we have looked at three principles that you can use when constructing an answering phrase:

1. **Repeat:** Use elements of the first phrase again, with a slight change.

2. **Develop:** Take an element from the first phrase and develop it. For example, if the first phrase starts with fast rhythms and then uses slower ones, do the opposite.

3. **Contrast:** Choose a rhythm that contrasts with the opening phrase.

Learn from the masters

One of the great advantages of being able to read music is that we can examine scores written by the great composers over the years and learn from them. So let's start by examining some famous classical melodies and trying to identify what makes them so memorable.

To start with, here's a phrase from Mozart's Eine Kleine Nachtmusik:

This phrase demonstrates both principles 1 and 2. From a rhythmic point of view, the second phrase is an exact repetition of the first phrase. However, if you look at the contour of phrase 1, you'll see that it moves upwards, whereas phrase 2 moves downwards.

Start here

Of course, there are many other factors to bear in mind when composing, but these three are a good place to start.

Online material

Visit **www.hybrid publications.com** to find other great pieces of classical music for you to analyse.

Let's look at another very famous piece of classical music – the opening to Beethoven's Fifth Symphony:

Here we can again see the principles of repetition and development at work. Beethoven starts with a catchy four-note motif (the famous da-da-da-da that we all know). This is immediately repeated – at a lower pitch, but the rhythmic pattern is identical. Then Beethoven develops the pattern by removing the space between the four-note motifs so that one follows on immediately after the other. Note too how the first two phrases move downwards, while the longer third phrase moves upwards, contrasting with the opening. Finally let's examine another of the most famous openings in classical music: J. S. Bach's Toccata and Fugue in D minor:

The piece opens with a dramatic three-note motif (an inverted mordent), which is answered by a downward phrase. Bach then returns to the opening motif, which is repeated exactly, an octave lower. This is then followed by a contrasting answering phrase. The combination of repetition and contrast produces a deeply satisfying musical effect. There are thousands of other examples that we could choose, not only from the world of classical music, but from popular music, folk music or other musical traditions from around the world. Try examining some of your favourite melodies and see if you can identify the principles of repetition, development and contrast at work.

Jargon buster

Motif
A short, melodic building-block of music
Phrase
A longer section of a melody, such as might be sung in one breath

Worksheet 8

1. Try composing answering rhythms to these opening rhythms using the principles discussed in this chapter.

Please note that there are no answers for this worksheet, as the answering rhythms that you write will not be 'right' or 'wrong', assuming that they obey the basic rules of music theory. Clap out the rhythms to a fellow musician and get them to assess how good they are and how they might be improved.

Chapter 9: Performance

This chapter is all about the different ways that musicians can interpret or embellish music to add interest. This might be through the way in which particular notes are styled or articulated, or it might be by adding decoration to a simple melody in order to create something more complex and interesting (in the same way that a carpenter might add some decorative touches to a plain chair leg, or an architect might add details to a flat structure). We're going to concentrate on specific types of decoration and ornamentation that have been used in western classical music, but it's worth remembering that similar principles are used in music of all types, from a guitar solo by Jimi Hendrix through to the traditional music of the Middle East or India.

Let's briefly recap of some of the elements of performance and articulation that we covered back in 'How To Read Music' and remind ourselves how they are written in music notation. Let's start with dynamics, the general term that musicians use to refer to how loudly or quietly they play. Dynamic levels can be specified using a series of abbreviations of Italian terms:

Dynamic level	Symbol	Italian term
Very quiet	pp	*pianissimo*
Quiet	p	*piano*
Quite loud	mf	*mezzo-forte*
Loud	f	*forte*
Very loud	ff	*fortissimo*

We can move between these flat dynamic levels using terms like *crescendo* (getting gradually louder) or *diminuendo* (getting gradually quieter – *decrescendo* is an alternative term). We use symbols called 'hairpins' to indicate crescendos and diminuendos:

Get it right

A phrase that's often used in spoken English is 'to reach a crescendo', meaning that something has arrived at a peak or maximum level. Of course, musicians will understand that the phrase is wrongly used, because a crescendo is a process of gradually getting louder, not something that one can 'reach' or arrive at.

Here's a brief summary of the most commonly-found articulation marks:

Name	Meaning	Symbol
Legato	smooth	
Tenuto	with a slight 'lean'	
Staccato	detached	
Stacatissimo	very detached	
Accent	accented	
Marcato	marked	
Sforzando	sudden increase in volume	

Tempo and mood

The speed of a piece of music is usually indicated at the start of the piece by a metronome mark (a metronome is a musical device that can be set to give different speeds, with the number indicating how many beats per minute):

Alternatively, a more generic descriptive term can be used (usually Italian) to give the performer a rough idea of the intended speed of the piece. A short list of the most commonly used terms is given here:

Adagietto	slow, but faster than adagio
Adagio	slow
Allegretto	fairly quick (but not as fast as allegro)
Allegro	quickly
Andante	at a walking pace
Andantino	either slightly slower or faster than andante
Doppio movimento	twice as fast
Grave	very slow
Langsam (Ger.)	slow
Largo	slow and stately
Lento	slow
Presto	fast
Vivace	quick

In addition, purely descriptive terms are often used to indicate the mood of the piece or the emotions that it is supposed to evoke:

Agitato	agitated
Anima	with feeling
Appassionato	passionately
Delicato	delicately
Dolente	mournful
Energico	energetic
Giocoso	playful
Grazioso	graceful
Lacrimoso	sad
Mesto	sad
Pesante	heavily
Piangevole	plaintive
Scherzando	jokingly
Tranquillo	calm
Triste	sad

Viva Italia!

Some musical terms are given in French, German, Spanish or even English, but the vast majority in common use are Italian. Note that the musical meanings of some of these phrases may differ from their strict current translations.

Online material

Visit **www.hybrid publications.com** to find a fuller list of music terms.

Grace notes and trills

In 'How To Read Music' we introduced two types of 'grace note', short additional notes that can be inserted before other notes. The first was the *appoggiatura*, the 'leaning note', which steals a bit of time from the note that follows it, and is written and played like this:

The amount of time that the *appoggiatura* 'steals' from the following note varies depending on whether the main note is dotted or not. In the above example, the main note is not dotted, and so the *appoggiatura* is allocated half the value of the main note.

However, if the main note is dotted then the *appoggiatura* is allocated two thirds of its value, like this:

Listen to **Audio track 25** to hear how this should sound.

Note that the rhythmic value used for the *appoggiatura* itself is not generally an indication of how much time should be allocated to it – for example, *appoggiaturas* can be written as small semiquavers, quavers or even crotchets, depending on the rhythmic context at the time, but the rules for how much time they occupy are still as outlined above.

Remember not to confuse the *appoggiatura*, which has a definite duration, with the *acciaccatura* (or 'crushed note'), which is squeezed in as closely as possible to the main note.

Top tip

Notice in this case that the grace note is actually longer than the 'main' note to which it is attached.

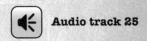

Audio track 25

Notation tip

In music notation a trill can be indicated by either the letters 'tr' or a horizontal wavy line, or both.

The trill (or shake) is, in its most basic form, a rapid alternation between the written note and the note above it. Up to (roughly) the year 1800, trills always began on the upper note, while after that date they more commonly began on the lower (written) note.

Trills also commonly include the note below the written note, in a little flourish right at the end of the trill:

Mordents and turns

There are two other common types of ornament that it is useful to familiarise yourself with. The first of these is the mordent, which comes in two 'flavours', the upper mordent and the lower mordent, written like this:

The mordent

The word 'mordent' is derived from the Latin verb *mordere*, which means 'to bite'.

The mordent is essentially just an instruction to move quickly from the written note to the note above or below and then back to the written note. In the upper mordent, you use the note above:

while in the lower mordent you use the note below:

 Ornament tip

The *auxiliary notes* in these ornaments (i.e. those above or below the main note) can be chromatically altered with sharps, flats or naturals if necessary.

The turn involves both the upper and lower notes, but varies in its effect depending on where the symbol is placed. In this example, the turn is placed directly over the note it relates to:

When positioned in this way, the turn should be played starting on the note above before moving to the written note, then the note below and finally returning to the written note. All the notes of the turn are given the same duration, with the exception of the last note, which can vary in duration. If the turn is written slightly between two notes, then the first written note should be played followed by the turn as described above, leading into the second note, like this:

The final possibility is that the turn is written after a dotted note, in which case the last note of the turn should occupy the duration indicated by the dot:

Slightly confusingly, there is another ornament called the inverted turn which looks almost identical to the turn. All the same rules apply, but instead of starting on the note above the written note, the inverted turn starts on the note below it.

Here's an example that uses trills, mordents and turns. Listen to **Audio track 26** to hear what these ornaments sound like.

The symbols used for ornaments are another type of musical shorthand; trained musicians understand exactly what each symbol means, thus removing the need for every single note to be written out. However, in some circumstances you may be asked to write out ornaments, which we'll deal with overleaf.

Making it up

In the Baroque era of music (roughly from 1600–1750) performers commonly added ornaments to melodies as a form of improvisation, a tradition that continues in the present day in folk and popular music.

Audio track 26

Writing out ornaments

Occasionally you may need to write out an ornament in full – perhaps when learning a new piece, or in one of your own compositions, or even when doing a music theory exam! Initially, this can be daunting, but a little common sense combined with the rules described on the previous pages is all you really need.

Let's start by looking at trills. Let's imagine that you are confronted with an example like this one and asked to write out (or 'realise') the ornament:

The first thing to look at is the speed of the piece, because the note value that we choose for the trill will inevitably be determined by the overall tempo; in a slow tempo you can fit a lot more notes into a crotchet than you can in a faster tempo. In this case, the tempo is *andante*, or walking pace and the duration of the note over which the trill is marked is a crotchet.

In this case, demisemiquavers seem like a reasonable choice – this will allow eight notes to be fitted into the duration of a crotchet. Our next question needs to be: when was this piece written? This will tell us whether the trill needs to start on the written note or on the note above it. In this case, let's assume that the piece was written prior to 1800, so that we need to start the trill on the upper note.

So, now we know that we can replace the trill with a set of eight demisemiquavers, starting on the note above the written note:

> ### Why bother?
>
> Remember, for pieces written pre-1800 the trill starts on the note above the written note. The only exception to this is if the trill is immediately preceded by the note above it. After 1800 the trill starts on the written note.

All we need to finish the trill off is a little 'turn' right at the end, where we move down to include the note below the trill, like this:

Andante

Mordents are even simpler as you don't have to worry whether to start on the note or not. All you need to do is to choose an appropriate note value for the three notes of the mordent. Again, this will be determined by the tempo, but perhaps to a lesser extent than the trill, because there are only three notes to be played.

So this phrase, which features both upper and lower mordents:

Allegretto

would be 'realised' like this:

Allegretto

Turns are perhaps the most complicated of the ornaments to write out, but even they are subject to just three basic rules: Firstly, if the turn symbol is written directly over the note then the ornament should start straight away on the upper note. Remember that the first three notes of the turn should all share the same note value. The fourth note might have the same note value, or it could be longer depending on the overall duration of the ornamented note and the tempo:

If the turn appears between two notes then we have two possibilities depending on whether the note that appears before the turn symbol is dotted or not.

If the first note is not dotted then the written note needs to be sounded first, before moving up to start the turn on the note above. Place the turn so that it leads directly into the second note:

If the first note is dotted then the procedure is exactly as described above except that you need to reserve enough time to allocate the value of the dot to the final note of the turn. In this case, the turn appears after a dotted crotchet, so we know that the final note of the turn has to be a quaver (the value of the dot). This then leaves us with a crotchet for the written note and the first three notes of the turn. Allocating a quaver to the written note and using a semiquaver triplet for the first three notes of the turn gives us a satisfactory realisation:

While this process of writing out ornaments can seem a little academic, it is great practice for your rhythmic notation and will really help you get used to using shorter note values. Try the exercises on the opposite page and on the worksheet on page 130 to test your knowledge.

Exercises

Write out the following trills:

Pre-1800

Post-1800

Write out this phrase again, using ornaments to simplify wherever possible:

Pre-1800

Pre-1800

Answers

Answers to all these exercises can be found at **www.hybrid publications.com**

Write out this turn in full:

Worksheet 9 (answers on page 166)

1. Match up these musical terms with their correct interpretations:

Dolente	playfully
Giocoso	mournful
Lacrimoso	heavily
Anima	with feeling
Pesante	sad

 Answers

Answers to this worksheet can be found on page 166.

2. Realise these ornaments:

 Online material

Additional worksheets are available at **www.hybrid publications.com**.

3. Prior to 1800, did trills begin on the upper or lower note?

4. In a slow tempo should you use longer or shorter note values when writing out ornaments?

Chapter 10: Harmony

In this chapter we're going to expand upon the basic introduction to harmony that formed the last chapter of 'How To Read Music'. Harmony is a huge area of music theory and has been the single subject of many books, so the information presented here is really only intended to be a taster. If it piques your interest then there is a whole world of harmony out there for you to explore.

Let's start by recapping the harmonised major scale, which can be created by stacking alternate notes from the major scale on top of one another to form triads. Here's the harmonised scale of C major:

You can hear how this sounds on **Audio track 27**. Because the pattern of notes in all major scales is the same, all harmonised major scales produce the same collection of major, minor and diminished triads. For example, here is the harmonised scale of G major:

In recognition of this fact, musicians use a Roman numeral system to identify the chords built on each degree of the major scale, allowing chord progressions to be specified independently of key. Upper case Roman numerals represent major chords while lower case numerals represent minor chords:

I	ii	iii	IV	V	vi	vii
major	minor	minor	major	major	minor	diminished

Audio track 27

Naming the dim

The diminished triad is given a lower case Roman numeral because it contains the interval of a minor third above its root, although it is not a minor triad.

Minor/major

Notice that in the harmonised minor scale the three most important triads (on degrees 1, 4 and 5) are all minor. In the harmonised major scale these triads are all major.

Harmonising the minor scale

Back on page 20 we harmonised the natural minor scale and we discovered that we got exactly the same collection of chords as we generated by harmonising the major scale, except in a different order. Hardly surprising when you consider that the natural minor scale contains exactly the same notes as the major scale, except in a different order:

i	ii	III	iv	v	VI	vii
minor	diminished	major	minor	minor	major	major

As you may recall, this gave us a problem because the all-important chord on the fifth degree is minor, not major, and therefore doesn't create the desirable 'pull' back to chord i.

This problem was solved by the creation of the 'harmonic minor' scale, with its sharpened seventh note, which becomes the major third of the V chord:

However, notice that the alteration of G to G sharp also affects two other chords in the harmonised scale. The chord built on the third degree of the natural minor scale is C major, and contains the notes of C, E and G. However, in the harmonised scale this has become C, E and G♯. Let's examine the intervals in this chord:

Bottom note to middle note: 4 semitones (*major 3rd*)
Middle note to top note: 4 semitones (*major 3rd*)
Bottom note to top note: 8 semitones (*augmented 5th*)

This is unlike any of the other chord types that we've encountered so far, being constructed from two major thirds on top of one another. Because the triad spans an augmented fifth it is known as an augmented triad. Another way of thinking of it is to imagine a major triad with the top note raised by a semitone.

The other triad that has changed as a result of the sharpened seventh is the chord built on the seventh degree itself, which has changed from a G major triad to a G♯ diminished triad.

So, the arrangement of chord types in the harmonised harmonic minor scale looks like this:

i	ii	III	iv	V	VI	vii
minor	diminished	augmented	minor	major	major	diminished

We've now encountered all four of the basic triads involved in traditional western harmony: the major, minor, diminished and augmented triads. These are the building blocks of all harmony in every genre, from classical music to blues, folk, or rock music.

Adding the seventh

Back in 'How To Read Music' we took the harmonisation of the major scale one step further and added another third on top of the basic triads to create a major scale harmonised in sevenths:

Cmaj7   Dm7   Em7   Fmaj7   G7   Am7   Bm7♭5   Cmaj7

Listen to **Audio track 28** to hear what this sounds like.

We have now created a selection of four-note chords:
major 7th (e.g. Cmaj7) = major triad plus a major seventh
minor 7th (e.g. Dm7) = minor triad plus a minor seventh
dominant 7th (e.g. G7) = major triad plus a 'natural' seventh
minor 7th flat 5 (e.g. Bm7♭5) = diminished triad plus a minor seventh

Let's see what happens if we do this to the natural minor scale.

Audio track 28

Keep it simple

chord naming conventions

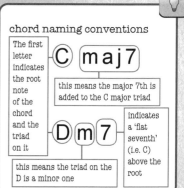

The first letter indicates the root note of the chord and the triad on it

this means the major 7th is added to the C major triad

this means the triad on the D is a minor one

indicates a 'flat seventh' (i.e. C) above the root

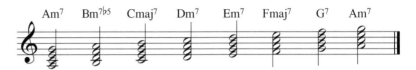

Audio track 29

Listen to **Audio track 29** to hear what this sounds like. Again, it shouldn't come as too much of a surprise to discover that the natural minor scale harmonised in sevenths contains exactly the same chords as the major scale, except in a different order. However, when we do the same thing to the harmonic minor scale we get some more interesting results:

Reminder

Refer back to page 20 for an explanation of the voice-leading in the V7-i cadence in a minor key.

Most crucially, the seventh chord built on the fifth degree of the scale is a dominant seventh, thus creating the perfect (V7-I) cadence that is the harmonic minor scale's *raison d'être*. But again, the presence of the raised seventh has some interesting effects, this time on the chords built on the root, third and seventh degrees.

The tonic chord, which was previously a minor seventh has changed because the G natural has changed to a G sharp, creating a new chord – a minor triad with a major seventh. Logically enough, this chord is known as A minor major seventh. It has an intriguing bitter-sweet sound, which you can hear on **Audio track 30**.

Audio track 30

The chord on the third degree, previously a C augmented triad, has gained a major seventh. This can be called C major 7th augmented, but is more commonly known as C major 7♯5, which is the same thing.

Cmaj⁷aug

Major 3rd   *Major 3rd*   *Minor 3rd*

The chord built on the seventh degree, which was previously a diminished triad, is even more mysterious. The distance from the bottom note to the top note is only nine semitones, one semitone smaller than any of the other chords in the harmonised scale, while the interval between each of its constituent notes is a minor third:

G♯dim⁷

Minor 3rd   *Minor 3rd*   *Minor 3rd*

This chord is known as the diminished seventh and its internal symmetry creates some interesting properties. Back in 'How To Read Music' we introduced the concept of 'inversions', versions of chords in which different notes are at the bottom of the chord. In most chords, different inversions create different 'flavours' of the chord, due to the different intervals created by re-arranging the order of the notes.

However, in the diminished seventh all the inversions have exactly the same symmetrical construction of four notes a minor third apart, so the different inversions all share the same 'flavour':

G♯dim⁷

Another interesting by-product of this symmetrical construction is that there are only three possible diminished seventh chords. Let's start with the diminished seventh from the harmonised A harmonic minor scale, G#dim7. If we transpose this up a semitone we can create another diminished seventh chord with its root on A. Repeating this process generates another diminished seventh chord on A#.

Key fact

The diminished seventh is often used as musical shorthand for suspense or drama. Just listen to the soundtracks to old silent movies and you'll hear it at key points of danger or tension.

If we try to repeat the process again we will create a diminished seventh chord with a root on B; however, this is simply an inversion of the G♯dim7 chord that we started with.

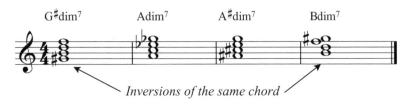

Inversions of the same chord

Because of this symmetrical inner structure, diminished seventh chords built on roots a minor third apart map exactly onto each other – hence there are only three individual diminished seventh chords possible. These two quirks alone make the diminished seventh chord a fascinating harmonic oddity and give it unique harmonic properties.

Exercises

Let's reinforce all this new information on harmony with some exercises. Start by trying to name these triads (if you get stuck, work out the intervals between the bottom and middle notes, and the middle and top notes, and then compare back with the triads that we've covered):

Now let's do the opposite; here you need to write the triads specified onto the stave.

Answers

Answers to these exercises can be found at **www.hybrid publications.com**

Now let's add in the sevenths and do the same thing. First, name these seventh chords taken from the harmonised C major scale:

Online material

Additional excercises on chord naming can be found at **www.hybrid publications.com**

Here are four sevenths from the harmonised A harmonic minor scale – see if you can name them:

Now try to construct the following seventh chords, which can all be found in the harmonised C major scale:

　　Em⁷　　　　　　G⁷　　　　　Fmaj⁷　　　　Am⁷

And now try the same thing for these four seventh chords from the harmonised A harmonic minor scale:

　　E⁷　　　　G♯dim⁷　　Am⁽ᵐᵃʲ⁷⁾　　Fmaj⁷

Answers

Answers to all these exercises can be found at **www.hybrid publications.com**

Now let's move outside the scales of C major and A minor, and see if you can apply your knowledge of chord construction to other keys. Start by building the triads indicated on the root notes given below:

　　E♭m　　　　Daug　　　　F♯　　　　B♭dim

Can you name these seventh chords?

And finally, construct the following seventh chords on the given root notes:

Dm(maj⁷) Fmaj⁷aug A♭m⁷ D♭maj⁷

Cadences

'Cadence' is a term that musicians apply to chords occurring at the end of a musical phrase. Cadences are the punctuation of music, they mark the end of phrases and help us to understand how they are constructed and what their musical meaning is. Like full stops, commas, semi-colons and the like, different cadences can create differing effects, bringing the music to a stop, pausing momentarily or driving onwards. There are four main types of cadence in common usage (although many others exist), and we've already introduced the first of these, the perfect cadence (back on page 19). At the risk of stretching the punctuation analogy too far, the perfect cadence is the musical equivalent of the full stop: it gives a sense of finality and completion to a phrase.

(back on page 19)

The perfect cadence consists of a major chord built on the fifth degree followed by the tonic chord. The chord on the fifth degree can be a simple major triad, or, for an even stronger effect it can be a dominant seventh:

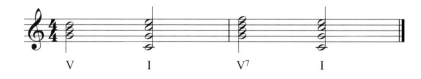

V   I   V⁷   I

Top tip

A movement from V-I is only called a perfect cadence if it occurs at the end of a phrase, and this applies to all other types of cadence as well.

As we saw back on page 19, the internal voice-leading of this cadence creates a deeply satisfying musical effect; the sensation is one of having 'arrived' on the tonic chord in a definitive sense.

An alternative to the perfect cadence is the *plagal* cadence, a move from chord IV to the tonic chord:

IV   I

The plagal cadence is also known as the 'Amen' cadence – you'll hear why if you listen to **Audio track 31**. Although the plagal cadence 'lands' on the tonic chord, it has a softer, less emphatic effect than the perfect cadence.

Not all cadences end on the tonic chord. For example, cadences that end on the dominant chord (the chord built on the fifth degree of the scale) are called *imperfect* cadences. In a sense, these cadences are the opposite of the perfect cadence, which moves from V to I. In imperfect cadences a number of chords can precede the dominant chord, the most common being I, IV and ii:

I   V   IV   V   ii   V

Listen to **Audio track 32** to hear what this sounds like. Because imperfect cadences deliver us to the dominant chord, they sound incomplete. Our ear wants to hear a return to the tonic chord, and so if we hear an imperfect cadence we instinctively expect there to be more music to come, to transport us from the dominant chord back to the tonic. For this reason, imperfect cadences often occur in the middle of phrases.

The final type of cadence we're going to look at is the *interrupted* cadence. This cadence tricks the ear into expecting a return to the

Audio track 31

Jargon buster

An alternative name for imperfect cadence is 'half cadence' or 'open cadence'.

Audio track 32

tonic chord, only to dash that expectation. The cadence is set up with a V chord, just like the perfect cadence, but instead of resolving to chord I it moves instead to the minor chord vi:

Of course, chords I and vi are closely related, but the effect of the interrupted cadence is to create a musical expectation, which is then denied, which can be very dramatic.

Cadences, keys and modulation

In addition to providing musical punctuation, cadences also perform an important musical function by contributing to our sense of key. In particular, the perfect cadence creates an incredibly strong sense of 'landing' on the tonic chord. This is because, in a major key, there is only one dominant seventh chord, and so moving from that chord to the tonic confirms to our ears exactly what the key is.

In fact, a single perfect cadence is usually enough to tell our ears that we have 'arrived' in a particular key. Composers exploit this property to allow them to move between keys within a single piece, or even within a phrase. This is known as *modulation*, and it's an important technique that allows composers to add interest, and avoid the monotony of a single key, especially in longer works.

Other cadences can also contribute to our sense of which key a piece is in, particularly those involving the V chord, but the perfect cadence is the primary tool that is used to establish the tonal centre, or key.

Space doesn't allow for an in-depth exploration of modulation here, but a simple example will suffice to demonstrate the concept. Take a look at the following musical example, which consists of two phrases, paying special attention to the cadences at the end of each phrase:

 Close to home

Most of the time, composers modulate to a key that is closely related to the original key – that is to say, one that is nearby on the circle of fifths (see page 27).

The ii-V-I

This cadence is also known as a ii-V-I, and is a staple of both classical music and jazz. It was famously used as the basis for George Gershwin's song 'I Got Rhythm' and is therefore known by jazzers as 'rhythm changes'.

Let's examine the cadence at the end of the first phrase. The harmony spells out the chords of G7 to C, a text-book perfect cadence. Note too the chord before the G7 – Dm7. The bass movement from D to G is a drop of a fifth, which is then followed by the rising fourth of G to C (an inverted fifth), adding to the finality of the cadence.

Down a fifth   Up a fourth

Now compare this with the cadence at the end of the second phrase, starting with the third chord from the end, an Em7. As we've seen, Em7 can be created by harmonising the C major scale (it's the chord built on the third degree of the scale). Another way of saying this is to say that it is *diatonic* to the key of C. However, Em7 is also diatonic to the key of D major, where it occurs on the second degree of the scale:

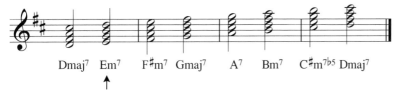

Dmaj⁷   Em⁷   F♯m⁷ Gmaj⁷   A⁷   Bm⁷   C♯m⁷ᵇ⁵ Dmaj⁷

This is known as a *pivot chord* – in other words it's a chord that exists both in the key that we are coming *from*, and in the key that we are moving *to*. As such it is tonally ambiguous; our ears will accept it as belonging to the key of C major, but it is not as definite as the dominant 7th chord, for example, which can only exist in one key.

The penultimate chord of the example is the first time that we hear a chord that is not diatonic to the key of C major – it's an A7 chord, with an alien C♯. In the key of C major, the chord built on a root note of A would be an A minor seventh, not a dominant seventh. Our ears pick up on this immediately – the fact that there is a root movement of a rising fourth (inversion of a fifth) from the previous chord of Em7 is also a warning sign that we might be about to modulate:

Up a fourth   Down a fifth

Now, A7 is only diatonic to one key, D major, where, as always, it occurs on the fifth degree of the scale:

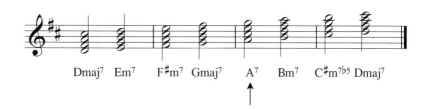

So, our suspicions of a shift in key, which were first aroused by the preceding Em7 chord, are furthered by this dominant chord, which adds further credence to a theory of a shift to D major.

The final confirmation arrives with the last chord of the example, the expected D major, making the A7-D move a perfect cadence in the new key of D major. We have now 'arrived' firmly in the new key and our ears hear D major as our new 'home' key.

Modulation can be far more subtle and skilful than this example, but the basic principles still apply. Listen out for modulations in the works of your favourite composers or songwriters and then examine how they have moved from one key to another.

Suspensions

We're going to finish this chapter on harmony with a brief look at a specific harmonic technique called a *suspension*. Let's start by re-examining the ii-V-I progression that we encountered in the previous section on modulation:

As we've seen this is a common cadential formula, and as such it can become a little tired and repetitive. One way of doing this is to leave one of the notes from the Dm7 chord 'hanging' on over the G7 chord, like this:

Notice how the C from the Dm7 chord is now included in the G7 chord – in fact, it has replaced the B note in the chord; if they were both included the semitone clash would be undesirable. The effect of this added note is to create tension – we can hear that the C doesn't 'belong' in the chord and our ears expect to hear the C fall back down to the B to give us the sound we expect. If we allow this to happen before moving on to the tonic chord we get a very pleasing effect:

Listen to **Audio track 33** to hear what this sounds like.

The C note that is held over from the Dm7 chord is said to be 'suspended' and the effect is called a *suspension*. The movement from the 'alien' C note to the expected B note is called the *resolution* – the suspension *resolves* from C to B.

The vertical chord that is created by the suspension is called a 'suspended 4th', because the C is the fourth degree of the G major scale:

So, this chord would be known as 'G7 suspended 4th' or G7sus4 for short.

Up or down?

Nearly all suspensions resolve downwards, with the exception of those where the suspended note is the leading note of the key, in which case it will resolve upwards to the tonic note.

There are a couple of rules that you need to observe when using suspensions. The first is that the suspended note has to be 'prepared'; this just means that it must appear in the chord immediately prior to the suspension. (It's worth noting that, while this rule is generally observed in classical music, in popular music 'sus4' chords are often used without any preparation at all.)

The second rule is that the suspension should not be sounded against the note that it is going to resolve to. So, in the example above, we removed the B note from the G chord, replacing it with the suspended C, which could then resolve back down to the B. If the B were already in the chord, the C would clash against it and the effect would be lost.

Think of suspensions having three parts – preparation, suspension and resolution. If we want to spice up our cadential progression further we can add another suspension between the G7 and C chords. This time we'll take the F note from the G7 chord and suspend it over the C chord – remember of course to remove the E note from the C chord so that it doesn't clash:

Listen to **Audio track 34** to hear what this sounds like.

Audio track 34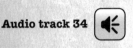

Double suspensions

Before we leave suspensions, we've just got space to look at one further technique, the double suspension. Let's take a look at a simple I-V-I progression:

As we've seen, this progression can be embellished with a suspension, like this:

Sus chords

'Suspended' chords are regularly used in popular music styles. These are chords in which the third of the chord has been replaced either by the second or the fourth degrees. These 'suspensions' may or may not be resolved.

So, here we have suspended the C note over the G chord, allowing it to resolve to B. However, we can go one step further here and also suspend the E note from the C chord, allowing it to resolve to D, as shown overleaf. For fairly obvious reasons, this is known as a *double suspension*.

Figured bass is a system used in the Baroque era, which specifies harmonies in relation to a given bass line. The numbers below the stave tell the performer which notes to add above the bass note. The number 6, for example, is an instruction to go up six scale steps, creating a first inversion major chord. Other than when playing Baroque music, figured bass isn't widely used, with modern musicians preferring to use chord symbols to describe this type of harmonic information.

The effect of this is to create a second inversion C chord that then moves to the dominant G. In classical music this is known as a six-four, five-three progression, which is how it would have been notated in figured bass:

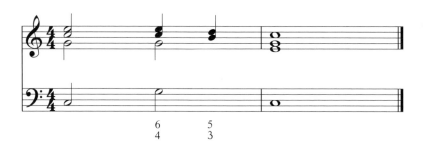

The 'six' and 'four' tell us to go up from the bass note, G, by six notes and four notes, giving us the E and A respectively, while the 'five' and the 'three' give us the D and B notes above the same bass note.

Further exploration

As we mentioned at the start of this chapter, harmony is a huge subject in music theory and all we have done here is to provide you with some of the basic concepts – we've really only scratched the surface.

Depending on your particular area of musical interest, there are several ways of continuing your exploration of the world of musical harmony. If the theoretical side appeals to you then there are several key text books on the subject, which will give you all the information you need (and then some).

However, a word of warning before embarking down this route: these books are serious academic tomes and can sometimes be impenetrable and rather daunting. A good place to start is *Harmony* by Walter Piston and Mark DeVoto, which will give you a thorough and comprehensive grounding.

If the academic route doesn't appeal, but you're still keen to gain an understanding of how harmony works, then there really is no substitute for studying music that you admire and figuring out how it works. A good local music teacher will be able to help and guide you in this process. While this may seem an expensive option, you will make much more rapid progress in this way, and he or she will be able to help you overcome 'roadblocks' or misunderstandings that could otherwise hold you up for months.

Start by finding a simple piece of music that appeals to you harmonically and try to track down the sheet music for it. If the piece you've chosen is a song, the sheet music may already have chord symbols on it, in which case half the job of understanding the harmony is done. If not, start with the bass line and try to analyse each chord in relation to the bass note. Remember that those chords that fall on the strong beats of the bar are usually the most important.

Talk through these chord progressions with your teacher or with another musician and try to apply some of the basic elements of harmony that we have introduced in this chapter. For example, you could start by analysing the chord changes at the end of musical phrases to see if you can identify the cadences that are used.

Good luck with your exploration – there's always something new to discover and you'll find that as you understand more about harmony works you'll appreciate and discover more great music than ever.

Further reading

Walter Piston's other two music textbooks – *Orchestration* and *Counterpoint* – are also considered essential reading for serious students of music theory.

Worksheet 10 (answers on page 167)

1. Name these chords, which are all taken from the harmonised scale of F major:

2. Write out these chords, which are all taken from the harmonised scale of A harmonic minor:

Answers

Answers to this worksheet can be found on page 167.

3. Name these cadences, in the key of E major:

4. Construct the following seventh chords on the given root notes:

5. Write out the other three inversions of this diminished seventh chord:

Chapter 11:
Composition (Part 2)

In this chapter we're going to revisit some of the principles that we discussed back in Chapter 8, where we looked at writing rhythmic patterns as 'answers' to given 'questions'. This time we're going to apply these principles to pitch as well as to rhythm, to allow you to try your hand at writing some answering melodies.

Before we can start writing melodies, we need to address the issue of which notes we can use to write them with. After all, not all notes will sound 'right' or pleasant. Remember, that within one octave we have the 12 notes of the chromatic scale to choose from, and within this collection of notes we have further groupings of notes into major and minor scales. As we've seen, all notes are not equal within a scale; some are more important than others, such as the tonic and the fifth degree.

So, in order to understand a melody, we need to know the key of the piece and therefore, the function of the notes of the melody in relation to that key. The key signature of any extract will give us a good idea of what the key is likely to be. So, for example in this case, a key signature of two sharps is likely to indicate either a key of D major or B minor:

Reminder

Refer back to pages 36–37 for a complete list of major and minor key signatures.

Having established two possible keys, we now need to look at the melody itself for further clues. Frequently, either the first or last notes of the melody will also be the root notes of the key, and in this case, both notes are D, so it is a fairly safe assumption that the key of this extract is D major. (Note, however, that it would still be possible, although unlikely, to harmonise this melody in B minor.)

Let's take a look at another example and apply the same techniques to see if we can establish its key...

In this case, we have no key signature. We have to be slightly careful here, because if there were a lot of accidentals, we might reasonably conclude that this extract has simply been written out without the correct key signature. However, in this case, we have only a solitary G# so it's safe to conclude that the key is either C major or A minor.

Examining the first and last notes of the melody, C and A respectively, doesn't really help us in this case. So, let's take another look at that G# note. If the extract were in C major, would we expect to find a G#? The answer is no – it's not part of the C major scale. Of course, it's not part of the A natural minor scale either, but it *is* part of the A *harmonic* minor scale – the sharpened seventh.

The fact that the G# moves immediately up to A is further evidence that points towards A minor as being the correct key for this piece.

So, having established the key of the opening phrase, we are now in a position to think about the note collections that we might use when constructing an answering phrase.

Writing answering melodies

Firstly, let's recap the three principles that you can use when constructing an answering phrase:

1. **Repeat:** use elements of the first phrase again, with a slight change

2. **Develop:** Take an element from the first phrase and develop it.for example, if the first phrase starts quickly and then slows down, do the opposite.

 Theory tip

Remember that in the major scale and in the harmonic minor scale there is only a semitone between the seventh note of the scale and the tonic. Our ears hear the 'leading note' as 'wanting' to resolve upwards to the tonic.

3. Contrast: choose a rhythm that contrasts with the opening phrase

Now let's apply these to a sample melodic phrase:

From the key signature and starting point of this melody, it should be fairly clear that it is in G major. So let's examine the given melody and see what characteristics or properties it has that we might be able to use in constructing our answering phrase.

Well, to start with, we can see that it opens with an ascending fragment of the G major scale. It also moves broadly upwards with some dotted note values towards the end.

In this case, let's invoke the principle of repetition and use a similar rhythm for our answering phrase. We can change our answering melody to develop and contrast with the opening phrase. Let's sketch in the rhythm (we have used a crotchet for the penultimate note to slow down the momentum of the tune):

Now to figure out where we want to begin and end the phrase. Let's start our phrase where the first phrase ended, and move back downwards to end on the root note, G. Let's put these notes in:

You can see that our answering melody is already starting to take shape – all that remains is us for to decide how to get from the beginning to the end!

Step one

When composing an answering phrase, your first step should always be to understand the qualities of the opening phrase. Only when you have done this can you hope to write an answering phrase that will be musically satisfying.

For the first bar of the answering phrase, let's use the same contour as we heard in the opening bar – because we're starting one note higher, the whole bar will therefore be one note higher – and let's repeat the second bar exactly as in the first phrase:

Now we don't have far to go to get to the final note of the phrase. In this part of the first phrase, notice how the notes move in a 'stepwise' fashion – each one is only one step away from the previous one and the next one; there are no big jumps. We might decide to do the same in our answering phrase, which would give a completed phrase looking something like this:

 Audio track 35

Listen to **Audio track 35** to hear what this answering phrase sounds like. This isn't the only possible answering phrase to this given opening – it's just one of many musically satisfying phrases that would work just as well (or maybe even better). Experiment yourself and see how many different phrases you can come up with.

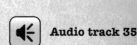 **Hearing voices**

Eventually, you will be able to look at a passage of written notation and hear how it will sound in your head, without even singing it out loud.

A great tip when trying to write melodies is to try singing the tune out loud. Try singing the opening phrase above and then just improvise an answering phrase and try to write down what you sang. Remember that a melody that is easy to sing is often going to be a musically satisfying one. You might well find that you come up with an answering phrase straight off the top of your head that works brilliantly – we all have an in-built sense of musicality and singing can be a great way to access this. This brings us nicely on to the next subject in this chapter, writing a melody to given words.

Writing a melody to given words

Music and language are intimately connected, and song has always been a vital part of human culture. So, composing melodies to words is an essential skill for any musician. Learning to do this expertly is a lifetime's study, and is far beyond the scope of this book. However, what we can do here is to examine some of the basic principles of setting words to music.

Broadly speaking there are two main principles to be aware of: rhythm and phrasing. Let's start by looking briefly at the rhythm of language and how we can relate it to musical rhythms.

Spoken language and words have a natural in-built rhythm. The way we each speak differs slightly, of course, but hard-wired into our language are certain rhythmic patterns – good word-setting relies on understanding these rhythms and writing melodies that work *with* them, rather than against them. Overlaid onto these rhythms are further patterns of stresses; some syllables of words are given more stress than others and again, it is our responsibility as musicians to try to reflect these stresses in the rhythms that we use when setting words to music.

Take for example the word 'apple' – how might we represent the rhythm of that word in musical notation. Perhaps, something like this:

ap - ple

Note that in the word 'apple' the stress falls on the first syllable: 'AP-ple', not 'ap-PLE', so we've put this pair of quavers *on* the beat. The first syllable then falls on the on-beat, with its stronger emphasis, while the less important second syllable falls on the off-beat, and therefore receives less stress.

Now, what about the word 'banana'? How might we represent that in notation?

Theory tip

Different languages have different patterns of stresses, and this accounts for some of the musical differences between composers from different countries.

Well, 'banana' has three syllables and the stress falls on the second syllable, like this: 'ba-NA-na'. So we need to allocate three notes to the word and put the second syllable on a strong beat, like this:

ba - na - na

And, finally continuing the fruit theme, what about 'watermelon'? Here we've got four syllables with the stress on the first syllable, so we might write something like this:

wa - ter - mel - on

So you can see that when presented with a phrase to set to music, we need to be aware of the number of syllables in each word, as well as where the stress falls. For example, if we were to take the phrase:

'I wandered lonely as a cloud'

our first job would be to figure out where the main stresses are. We might conclude that they fall like this:

I <u>wan</u>-dered <u>lone</u>-ly as a <u>cloud</u>'

This tells us that when we compose our melody, these words should fall on the strong beats of the bar. A possible rhythm for these words might look something like this:

I   wan-dered lone-ly   as   a cloud

Feed the meter

Most poems have a particular 'meter', or pattern of word stresses. Try to recognise this and choose a time signature that fits with the meter of the poem.

The second line of Wordsworth's poem is:
"That floats on high o'er vales and hills'

which, if we mark the stresses, looks like this:
"That <u>floats</u> on <u>high</u> o'er <u>vales</u> and <u>hills</u>'

Now, because this is a poem, each line has a very similar rhythm, which means we can use the same rhythmic pattern for the second line as for the first:

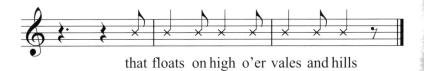

At this point we need to consider the phrasing of our melody; we have two separate musical rhythms that need to be joined together. Remember that we are writing a melody to be sung, and that the singer will need space to breathe at regular intervals. Remember too that the music itself needs space to 'breathe' – we don't want relentless singing with no gaps or pauses, so we need to bear this in mind when stitching our two phrases together. So, the rhythm of the first two lines might look something like this:

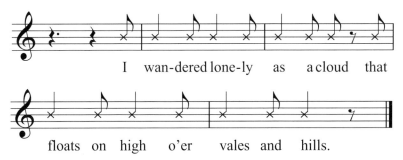

Mind the gap

Even if you're writing a melody that's not going to be sung, it's still important to leave gaps, so that the music has room to 'breathe'.

Note the rest that separates the two lines, giving the singer room to breathe if necessary (although both these phrases could probably be sung in one breath), but also allowing musical space in the rhythm. All that remains is for us to add pitch to this rhythm and we have created a melody.

Here's are the first two lines of Wordsworth's poem set to music:

I wan-dered lone - ly

as a cloud that floats on high o'er vales and hills.

 Audio track 36

Listen to **Audio track 36** to hear what this sounds like. Again, the usual caveat applies – this is only one possible interpretation of how to set these words to music. There are probably an infinite number of alternative ways of doing it that are as good as, or better than this, so why not have a go yourself?

Exercises and ideas

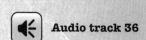

There's no worksheet at the end of this chapter because, as pointed out above, there are really no right and wrong answers when it comes to setting words to music. However, what follows are some ideas for sources of lyrics that you might like to try setting to music as well as some other suggestions to give you inspiration.

Remember too that there is no substitute for singing your melodies out loud – this is the ultimate acid test for any tune. If you feel that you can't sing or are self-conscious about your own voice then get a friend to come in and sing them for you. They'll soon tell you if they are comfortable and enjoyable to sing.

1. Write your own! Writing your own lyrics can often be the easiest way to get into the world of writing melodies. You can write about subjects that interest you, in a way that you find appealing, and you may even have a pre-formed melody in mind.

Keep it simple

In composition, as in many things, there is often a temptation to over-complicate things. Remember that often the simplest solution is the best.

2. Check out your favourite poets. Whether it's Shakespeare or Ginsberg, poems are a great source of material to practise word-setting. Because most poems, like music, have a meter, they are perfect for setting to music. Experiment with poets from different eras, and even different languages!

3. Learn from the masters. Choose a text that has already been set to music by your favourite composer or songwriter. Have a go at creating your own melody and then compare back to see what your chosen songwriter/composer did with the same material. Another interesting exercise is to find material that has been used by more than one composer and compare how differently it was treated.

4. Learn from other musicians. Why not get together with friends and collaborate on setting some words to music? Or why not work with a friend – one of you can write the words and the other writes the music. Then swap over and do it the other way round. Many of the most famous songs in the world have been written by songwriting partnerships, so why not give it a go?

5. Listen, listen listen! There really is no substitute for listening to as much music as you can. Don't restrict yourself to one style or genre either, make the effort to seek out interesting writing in areas that you're not so familiar with. So, if you're a fan of Bach and Vivaldi, why not check out the songwriting of George Gershwin or Jerome Kern? If your thing is blues then explore the songs of Debussy. Take yourself outside your comfort zone and you're bound to learn something.

Congratulations

If you've worked through this book you should, by now, have a comprehensive knowledge of music theory. We've covered the whole gamut of music theory including notation, harmony, composition and general musicianship, but the emphasis has always been on putting this theory into practice. Whatever your taste in music, whatever instrument you play and whether or not you write your own music, I can assure you that as a musician you will use this information on a daily basis.

So well done, and congratulations on getting this far. Remember that there is a lot more material for you to get your teeth into on the website at **www.hybridpublications.com** so head over there to download extra worksheets and access the other goodies.

Lifelong learning

Of course, everything we have learned up to this point is only the beginning of a long voyage of musical discovery. No matter how much you know as a musician there is always more to discover, more to understand and there are always other musicians to meet and learn from. The study of music really is a lifelong process, and the best musicians are those that continue to seek out new knowledge and musical insight as they develop.

There are many other tuition and theory books out there that will give you much more detailed information about your particular area of interest; check out **www.musicroom.com** for a comprehensive selection. They also stock a massive range of sheet music, so whether you want to brush up on your sight-reading or just learn the chords to your favourite song, they'll have something for you.

Good luck and keep learning!

Worksheet 1 – ANSWERS

1. Write out the scales of F major (on the treble stave below) and
E major (on the bass stave below). Don't use a key signature – use
accidentals where necessary:

2. Write out the scales of G natural minor (on the bass stave below)
and F natural minor (on the treble stave below). Don't use a key
signature – use accidentals where necessary:

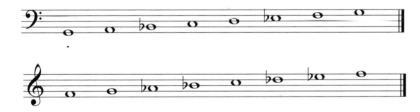

3. Write out the scales of B harmonic minor (on the bass stave
below) and D harmonic minor (on the treble stave below). Don't use a
key signature – use accidentals where necessary:

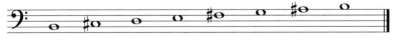

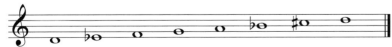

Worksheet 2 – ANSWERS

1. Write out the scales of E♭ major (on the treble stave below) and B major (on the bass stave below). Use the correct key signatures in each case.

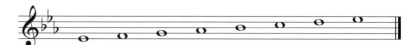

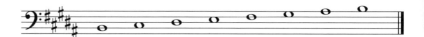

2. Write out the scales of F harmonic minor (on the treble stave below) and C harmonic minor (on the bass stave below). Use the correct key signatures in each case.

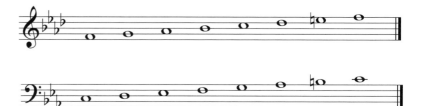

3. Various double sharps and double flats are written on the stave below – next to each one write its enharmonic equivalent without the use of accidentals.

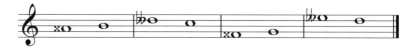

4. Write enharmonic equivalents of the following notes using

Worksheet 3 – ANSWERS

1. Try writing this example in 4/4 again in 2/4, doubling the speed of every note:

2. Try writing this example in 4/4 again in 4/2, halving the speed of every note:

3. Write out this example in 12/8 in 4/4, using triplets where necessary:

4. How many demisemiquavers could be fitted into one breve?

A: 64

Worksheet 4 – ANSWERS

1. Write the letter names of these notes under the stave:

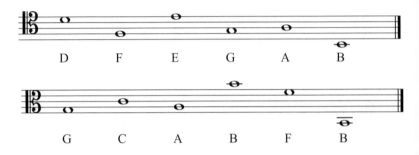

2. Write these notes on the alto and tenor staves below, using up to one ledger line. Remember that some notes can be found in more than one place:

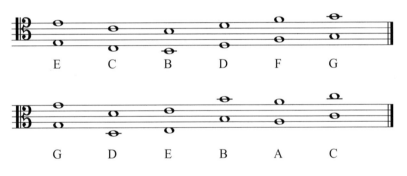

3. Copy this passage into the bass clef:

4. Which clef is used mainly by the viola?

A: The Alto clef

Worksheet 5 – ANSWERS

1. Transpose this melody down an octave, putting it into the tenor clef:

2. Transpose this melody up a major third:

3. Transpose this melody up a perfect fifth and into the treble clef:

4. For each instrument, the given note represents the sounding pitch – in each case, add the written pitch that would result in this sounding note next to it.

Clarinet   Oboe   Trumpet   Horn

Worksheet 6 – ANSWERS

1. Add beams to this example in 9/8:

2. Add beams to this example in 5/8 to show a subdivision of 3+2:

3. Write out this melody in 6/16, halving each note value:

4. Which of these is not an irregular time signature?
5/4, 7/8, 9/8, 11/16

A: 9/8

Worksheet 7 – ANSWERS

1. How many strings do instruments in the String family of instruments have?

A. Four

2. What is the lowest member of the String family?

A. Double Bass

3. Join up these Italian string techniques with their correct English counterparts:

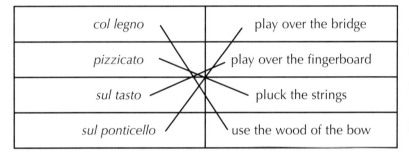

col legno	play over the bridge
pizzicato	play over the fingerboard
sul tasto	pluck the strings
sul ponticello	use the wood of the bow

4. Which of these is a double reed instrument?

A. Trumpet

B. Oboe

C. Viola

D. Flute

5. Join each instrument up with its correct key:

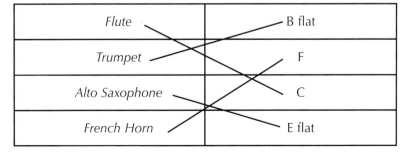

Flute	B flat
Trumpet	F
Alto Saxophone	C
French Horn	E flat

6. How many strings does a guitar have?

A. Six

Worksheet 9 – ANSWERS

1. Match up these musical terms with their correct interpretations:

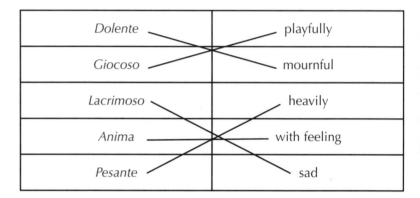

2. Realise these ornaments:

3. Prior to 1800, did trills begin on the upper or lower note?
A: They began on the upper note.

4. In a slow tempo should you use longer or shorter note values when writing out ornaments?
A. You should use shorter note values.

Worksheet 10 – ANSWERS

1. Name these chords, which are all taken from the harmonised scale of F major:

     Am⁷   Gm⁷   Fmaj⁷   Em⁷ᵇ⁵

2. Write out these chords, which are all taken from the harmonised scale of A harmonic minor:

     Bm⁷ᵇ⁵   Fmaj⁷   Cmaj⁷aug   Am⁽ᵐᵃʲ⁷⁾

3. Name these cadences, in the key of E major:

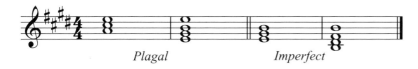

       Plagal   *Imperfect*

4. Construct the following seventh chords on the given root notes:

     F♯maj⁷   Em⁽ᵐᵃʲ⁷⁾   Dᵇ⁷   Eᵇm⁷

5. Write out the other three inversions of this diminished seventh chord:

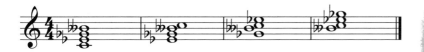

Index

A minor scale 16, 18, 21, 37
accents 118
accidentals 11–12
    and scales 14–15
    and transpositions 66–7
    see also flats; sharps
acoustic guitars 104–5
Aeolian mode 16
altissimo register 98
alto clef 53–4, 57, 58
alto voices 58, 60, 61
ascending intervals 13
augmented 4th interval 13
    and perfect cadence 19, 20
augmented triads 131, 132

B minor scale 17, 28, 37
Bach, J.S., Toccata and Fugue in D minor 115
baritones 60
Baroque music 123, 141, 144
bass clef 11, 51, 52, 58
bass guitars 106
bass voices 58
bassoons 55, 57, 58, 97, 99
beams, in irregular time signatures 88, 89
Beethoven, Ludwig, Fifth Symphony 115
brass instruments 92, 100–2
    cornets 75
    French horns 99, 101
    mutes for 100
    pitch 100
    `taps' in 100
    trombones 55, 57, 58, 100, 102
    trumpets 58, 71, 72, 73, 74, 75, 100, 101
        piccolo trumpet 101
    tubas 58, 102
breves 42–3, 48

C major scale 13–14, 16, 36
    harmonised 18, 129, 139
    perfect cadence 19
cadences 136–40
    imperfect (half or open) 137
    interrupted 137–8
    keys and modulation 138–40
    perfect 19–20, 23, 136–7, 138
    plagal 137
    suspensions 141–4
call and response 112
cellos 55, 57, 58, 96
chalameau register 98

chords
    guitar chord symbols 107
    pivot chords 139
    and string instruments 95
    see also harmony
chromatic scale 12–13, 28
circle of fifths
    major keys 27–8
    minor keys 29
clarinets 58, 70, 71, 73, 74, 75, 97, 98
    registers 98
classical melodies, and composition 114–15
clefs 11, 51–62
    alto (C clef) 53–4, 57, 58
    bass (F clef) 11, 51, 58
    and ledger lines 11, 51–2
    and open scores 60–1
    tenor 55–6, 57, 58
    and transpositions 52, 58, 64–5, 69
    treble (G clef) 11, 51, 52, 53, 57, 58
    and voice types 60–1
common time 77, 83
composition 111–16
    call and response 112
    and classical melodies 114–15
    repeat, develop and contrast 114, 115,
        148–50
    retrograde 113
    writing melodies 147–55
        to given words 151–4
compound time 49, 78–82, 86
    grouping notes in 79–81
    rests in 81–2
computer software, and transposition 64, 69
concert pitch 72, 74
contrabassoons 99
cor anglais 99
cornets 75
counter-tenors 60
crescendo 117
crotchet rests 39, 48
crotchets 39, 44, 48
cut common time 77, 83
cymbals 103, 108

D major scale 15, 25, 36
decrescendo 117
demisemiquavers 41, 43, 48
descending intervals 13
diminished 4th interval 13
diminished seventh chords 133–4

diminished triads 129, 131, 133
diminuendo 117
dotted notes 40
    grouping in compound time 81
    turns written after 123, 126
dotted rests 82
double bass 57, 58, 96
double sharps/flats 34
    cancelling 35
double suspensions 143–4
drums
    orchestral 103
    rock and pop music 108–9
duple time signatures 83
duplets 45–7, 49

E minor scale 17, 21
Egyptian music 21
electric guitars 104–5
electronic keyboards 109
enharmonic equivalents
    double sharps and flats 34
    major keys 27
    minor keys 30–3
euphonium 57

F major scale 22, 36
figured bass 144
flats 11, 12
    and the chromatic scale 12
    double 34
        cancelling 35
    flat key signatures 15, 26–7, 28
flutes 58, 73, 97, 98, 100
French horns 99, 101

G major scale 14, 17, 25, 36
    harmonised 129
G minor scale 22, 37
Gershwin, George 139
Glennie, Evelyn 103
glockenspiels 103
gongs 103
grace notes 120
guitars 58, 75
    acoustic 104–5
    bass 106
    capos 66, 105
    electric 104–5
    notation 106–7
    plectrums 105

half cadences 137
harmonic minor scale 21–2, 23, 130–1, 148

enharmonic equivalents 30–3
harmony 129–46
    books on 144–5
    cadences 19–20, 23, 136–40
    harmonised major scale 129
    harmonised minor scale 18, 130–1, 131–4
    seventh chords 131–6
    suspensions 141–4
history of music 91

imperfect cadences 137
instruments 91–110
    orchestral 91–103
    rock/pop bands 104–9
    specialist 104
    transposing 70–5
interrupted cadences 137–8
intervals 12–13
    inversions 27
inversions 27
irrational time signatures 86
irregular time signatures 86–9
    beams and ties in 88–9

jazz bands 102
jazz flutes 98

key signatures 15, 17, 25–38
    circle of fifths 27–8
    enharmonic equivalents 27
    major scales 15, 25–8, 36
    and melodies 147–8
    minor scales 28–9, 37
    and transpositions 66–7
    see also flats; sharps
keyboard instruments, pop and rock groups 109
keys 14–15
    and modulation 138–40
KISS (Keep it Simple, Stupid) 80

language, writing melodies to given words 151–4
leading notes 14
ledger lines 11, 51–2
legato 40, 79, 118

major scales 13–15, 36, 148
    circle of fifths 27–8
    harmonised 129
    intervals 13
    key signatures 15, 25–8, 36
    and minor scales 16–17
    and modulation 140
    perfect cadence 19
marcato 118

marimbas 103
Marsalis, Wynton 101
math rock 78
melodic minor scales 23, 37
metronomes 118
mezzo-sopranos 60
microtones 35
Middle C 11
minims 39, 44, 48
　counting in 83
minor scales 16–24, 37
　circle of fifths 29
　enharmonic equivalents 30–3
　harmonic 21–2, 23, 30–3, 130–1, 148
　harmonised 17–18, 130–1
　　in sevenths 131–4
　intervals 13
　key signatures 28–9, 37
　melodic 23, 37
　and modulation 140
　natural 16–17
　　harmonised in sevenths 131–2
　perfect cadence 20
　relative minor 20, 28
modes 16
modulation 138–40
mordents 121–2, 125
motifs 115
Mozart, W.A., *Eine Kleine Nachtmusik* 114
mutes
　for brass instruments 100
　for string instruments 94

natural minor scale 16–17
　harmonised 17–18, 130
naturals 11, 12, 15
note values 39–45, 48
　breves 42–3, 48
　crotchets 39, 44, 48
　demisemiquavers 41, 43, 48
　dotted notes 40
　minims 39, 44, 83, 85
　quavers 39, 44–5, 48
　semibreves 39, 48
　semiquavers 39, 44, 48, 85
　tied notes 40
　UK and US names 39, 42
　see also rest values

oboes 58, 74, 97, 99
octaves 12, 13
　transposition 52, 57, 63–5
open cadences 137
open scores 60–1

orchestral instruments 91–103
　brass 92, 100–2
　organisation of the orchestra 92
　percussion 92, 103
　string 92, 93–6
　woodwind 92, 97–9
Oriental music 21
ornaments 120–3
　writing out 124–8

percussion instruments 92, 103
perfect cadences 19–20, 23, 136–7
　in major keys 19
　in minor keys 20, 23
　and modulation 138
perfect intervals 13
performance 117–28
　articulation marks 118
　dynamic levels 117
　ornaments 120–8
　tempo and mood 118–19
phrases (in a melody) 115
piccolo trumpets 101
piccolos 75
Piston, Walter 145
pitched percussion instruments 103
pivot chords 139
plagal cadences 137
poetry, setting to music 151–4, 155
popular music, instruments 104–9

quaver rests 39, 48, 82
quavers 39, 48
　triplets 44–5

recorders 97
resolution 142
rest values 39, 40, 41, 48
　breve rest 43
　in compound time 81–2
　in irregular time signatures 88
　and triplets 45
rhythmic notation 39–50
　composition 111–13
　dotted 40, 48
　duplets 45–7, 49
　guitars 107–8
　note values 39–45, 48
　ties 40, 48, 79
　triplets 44–5, 47
　tuplets 44, 49
rock music
　instruments for pop and rock 104–9
　math rock 78

saxophones 71, 72, 73, 75, 97, 100
scales *see* major scales; minor scales
semibreve rests 39, 48, 81
semibreves 39, 48
semihemidemisemiquavers 41
semiquavers 39, 41, 44, 48
    counting in 85
semitones
    and intervals 13
    major scale 13–14, 16
    minor scale 16–17
sforzando 118
sharps 11–12
    double 34
        cancelling 35
    half sharps 35
    sharp key signatures 15, 25–6, 27, 28
    three-quarter sharps 35
simple time signatures 49, 77–8, 85
slurs 40, 79
soprano voices 58, 60, 61
staccatissimo 118
staccato 40, 118
staves 11, 52
    drums 108–9
    guitar tab 107–8
    ledger lines 11, 51, 52
    upper and lower voices 61
    see also clefs
Stradivarius, Antonio 93
string instruments 92, 93–6
    bows 93
    cellos 55, 57, 58, 96
    and chords 95
    double bass 57, 58, 96
    mutes 94
    pitch 93
    techniques 94
    tuning 94
    violas 53, 57, 58, 95
    violins 58, 95
suspensions 141–4

tablature 106–8
tempo 118–19, 124
tenor clef 55–6, 57, 58
tenor voices 58, 60, 61
tenuto 118
ties 40, 79
    grouping in compound time 80–1
    in irregular time signatures 88, 89
time signatures 77–90
    and the breve 42–3
    common time 77, 83
    compound 49, 78–82, 86

counting in minims 83–4, 85
counting in semiquavers 85
cut common time 77, 83
and duplets 45–6
irrational 86
irregular 85–9
regular 85
simple 49, 77–8, 85
timpani 103
tonal centres 138
tones
    major scale 13–14
    minor scale 16–17
tonic chord 132, 136, 137, 138
transposition 63–76
    instruments 70–5
    non-octave 66–9
    octaves 52, 57, 63–5
treble clef 11, 51, 52, 53, 57, 58
trills 121, 124–5
triplets 44–5, 47
trombones 55, 57, 58, 100, 102
trumpets 58, 71, 72, 73, 74, 75, 100, 101
    piccolo trumpet 101
tubas 58, 102
tubular bells 103
tuning
    electric guitars 105
    string instruments 94
tuplets 44, 49
turns 122–3
    writing out 125–6

unison 13

vibraphones 103
violas 53, 57, 58, 95
violins 58, 95
voice types, and clefs 60–1
voice-leading, and perfect cadence 19, 20

woodwind instruments 92, 97–9
    bassoons 55, 57, 58, 97, 99
    clarinets 58, 70, 71, 73, 74, 75, 97, 98
    cor anglais 99
    flutes 58, 73, 97, 98
    oboes 58, 74, 97, 99
    recorders 97
    saxophones 71, 72, 73, 75, 97, 100
    single- and double-reed 97

xylophones 103

Zappa, Frank 111

This companion edition is also available...

The authors of *How To Crack Music Theory* have also produced this essential guide to reading and writing music.

Written in easy-to-understand plain English, it is supplemented by audio material and other extras all available online at hybridpublications.com

This means that you get lots of examples of how things should sound plus many online bonuses, all clearly flagged on the relevant page in the book. Like *How To Crack Music Theory*, regular worksheets at the chapter ends ensure you have understood the key points before moving on.

Book with access to complementary website: Order No. AM986887

Still available...
Helen Cooper's classic guide
to the basics of reading music

Even if you have never read a note of music before, this book will teach you how – easily and quickly. If you could once read music but have forgotten how, this book will quickly refresh your memory.

- Contains every term and sign you are likely to come across when studying music.

- Ideal for classroom and private teaching of the rudiments of music.

- Essential if you are learning an instrument or learning to sing.

The book is also available with a CD containing 24 musical illustrations of many of the written music principles covered in each section of the book.

Book only: Order No. OP41904
Book & CD: Order No. AM91452

Bringing you the words and the music

All the latest music in print...
rock & pop plus jazz, blues, country,
classical and the best in West End
show scores.

- Books to match your favourite CDs.

- Book-and-CD titles with high quality
  backing tracks for you to play along to.
  Now you can play guitar or piano with your
  favourite artist... or simply sing along!

- Audition songbooks with CD backing
  tracks for both male and female singers
  for all those with stars in their eyes.

- Can't read music? No problem, you can
  still play all the hits with our wide range of
  chord songbooks.

- Check out our range of instrumental
  tutorial titles, taking you from novice to
  expert in no time at all!

- Musical show scores include *The Phantom
  Of The Opera*, *Les Misérables*, *Mamma
  Mia* and many more hit productions.

- DVD master classes featuring the
  techniques of top artists.

Visit your local music shop or, in case of difficulty, contact the Marketing Department,
Music Sales Limited, Newmarket Road, Bury St Edmunds, Suffolk, IP33 3YB, UK
marketing@musicsales.co.uk

1 2 3 4 5 6 7 8 9